The Play
of
The Goalkeeper's Revenge

DEREK NICHOLLS
and
RAY SPEAKMAN

from the writings of
BILL NAUGHTON

HEINEMANN
LONDON

Heinemann Educational Books Ltd
22 Bedford Square, London WC1B 3HH

LONDON EDINBURGH MELBOURNE AUCKLAND
HONG KONG SINGAPORE KUALA LUMPUR
NEW DELHI IBADAN NAIROBI JOHANNESBURG
EXETER (NH) KINGSTON PORT OF SPAIN

British Library Cataloguing in Publication Data

Nicholls, Derek
  The play of The goalkeeper's revenge.
  I. Title II. Speakman, Ray III. Naughton, Bill.
  The goalkeeper's revenge
  822'.914   PR6064.I/
  ISBN 0-435-23724-1

Typeset by The Castlefield Press of Northampton
and printed and bound in Great Britain by
Spottiswoode Ballantyne of Colchester and London

PRODUCTION NOTES

We were delighted when Bill Naughton gave us permission to adapt part of his prose fiction for performance on the stage by The Birmingham Youth Theatre. We had known the two collections of short stories, *The Goalkeeper's Revenge* and *Late Night on Watling Street*, for a number of years, and we loved their way of celebrating people's quirks and peculiarities, and their sudden shafts of gentle compassion. Lying behind the stories, especially the childhood ones set in Bolton, was the vanished way of life of the ginnels, gable ends and blackened terraces of the nineteen-twenties and -thirties. Reading in preparation for this play introduced us to two stunning works — the autobiography *A Roof Over Your Head* with its stark pictures of absolute poverty and unemployment before the Welfare State, and the novel *One Small Boy*, which is a multi-coloured patchwork about the joys and sorrows of childhood — a knockout for both of us. We also discovered one of his children's books, *My Pal Spadger*.

The play draws on all of these books — not just on the collection called *The Goalkeeper's Revenge*. If you compare the script with the original stories, you will often find that we have changed the names of the characters. For instance, in A REAL GOOD SMILE, we changed Billy's friend and neighbour who instructs him in how to approach Mr. Bidwell from Alf to Spadger. There are many other examples. The principal character of the play is Bill — but the principal character of *One Small Boy* is Michael.

This was part of our solution to the problem of turning a number of different stories into a play. We decided to build it around one central character — and it must be obvious why we decided to call him Bill. In order to build up some of the friendships in Bill's life, we made other changes. Charlie Criddle, for instance — a character from the novel *One Small Boy* — seemed to be just the right boy to tell the story about the lion in A GOOD SIXPENN'ORTH. In this way it was possible to give continuity to Bill's life as it unfolded in the play.

The structure of the play is quite simple. Act One is about childhood and school days — friendships, betrayals, disappointments, secrets, adventures. Act Two is about the bridge between childhood and adulthood, and concentrates on early experiences at work — successes, failures, decisions about the future, and a deepening understanding of friendship.

Again and again the play returns to 'the street corner' or 'the gable end', where jokes were cracked, gossip exchanged, tall stories were told. Before radio and television, these street-corner tales were a kind of window looking out on life.

Bill Naughton is above all a storyteller — and this is the approach we adopted in the play. It is all based, one way or another, on storytelling: Charlie's story which earns him half-a-crown; Felix's tall stories about oranges and fishing; Spadger's stories of pit life; Hetty's story to Bill about her child-to-be — and so on. All of it forms the story of Bill's early life.

The play is largely episodic, and has over twenty scenes. It is perfectly possible to omit some of them completely, and groups wishing to produce the play may want to do so, to simplify staging and casting.

Simple staging is essential. If the costumes are carefully chosen to be as authentic as possible, the stage, filled with its many characters, will suggest location and atmosphere. The more smoothly the play flows from one situation to another — without massive scene-changes — the better.

In the original production, the set (designed by students from Birmingham Polytechnic School of Theatre Design) was a black box with 'appliqué' details of Bolton life — a pit wheel; a suggestion of slate roofing; a chimney; and so on. The furniture (tables and stools) were black and simple, and on the set all the time, to blend with the general suggestion of a landscape. The chairs and tables could rapidly be arranged as needed by the actors — those in the previous scene, or some brought on stage specially. Stage management was never seen on stage. The furniture was, at various times, the rows of desks in the school; benches in the mill; furniture in Spadger's house, and so on — always, however, being the bare essentials.

In A BIT OF BREAD AND JAM, Felix, Bill and Sammy mimed the fishing tale — casting in; catching fish; finding the loose board in the fence; sitting in the ambulance, etc. — as they told it. They were joined by other actors who impersonated Mr. Pratt, the policeman, and Bill's mother (amusingly played by a boy).

In ON THE MOORS, the suggestion of moorland came from the lighting, and from what we saw Bill and Ella apparently looking at and responding to — a principle to adopt throughout the play.

iv

The first production of THE GOALKEEPER'S REVENGE was performed by The Birmingham Youth Theatre at Birmingham Repertory Theatre Studio Theatre in January 1982; at Midlands Arts Centre, Birmingham, in March 1982; and at the Sunday Times National Student Drama Festival at Hull University in April 1982.

The Play of the Goalkeeper's Revenge draws on the following works of Bill Naughton: *The Goalkeeper's Revenge, A Good Sixpenn'orth, A Bit of Bread and Jam, A Real Good Smile* and *Weaver's Knot* (short stories); *One Small Boy* and *My Pal Spadger* (novels); *A Roof Over Your Head* (autobiography).

SYNOPSIS OF SCENES

CHARACTERS IN ORDER OF SPEAKING

BILL

SPADGER CHADWICK
FELIX
ERNIE HADDOCK
JIMMY
PONGO
SAMMY FEATHERS

Friends who live in Bolton. At the beginning of the play, all except Spadger are at the same Roman Catholic school. Spadger, Felix and Ernie are slightly older.

BOB THROPPER	Centre forward for Bolton Wanderers
CHARLIE CRIDDLE	A close schoolfriend of Bill
THE GREAT WALDO	A fairground liontamer
LADY	Waldo's assistant
SIM DALT	The Goalkeeper, who gets his revenge
MISS TWINING	A teacher, standing in for Fat Ada, who is sick
MAJOR PLANT	An Inspector of Schools
NORMAN TRIBLEY	A dunce at mathematics
ROSIE BEARDSON	A domineering girl
ELLA SHARLEY	Who becomes Bill's girlfriend
PHYLLIS GIRLS 1 and 2	Friends of Rosie and Ella
HERBERT	Another Bolton lad
BASHER	And another
NIGHTSOILSMEN 1 and 2	
MICHAEL	Bill's elder brother
TOMMY	Another Bolton lad
BOYS 1 and 2	Older boys
POLICE CONSTABLES 1 and 2	
LADY 1 (voice offstage)	The Squire's wife
LADY 2	A farmer's wife
HOUSEHOLDER	
WOMAN	Who buys coal from the coal-pickers
BILL'S FATHER (voice offstage)	
MAN	Who sweeps Mr. Bidwell's office
MR. BIDWELL	Manager at the Locomotive Works
HETTY	A weaver, in her early thirties
EDDIE HAMBULL	Weaving shed foreman
DELIA GIRL	Weavers
DOCTOR (female)	
SPADGER'S MOTHER	
LAD	Who has won a book as a prize

ACT ONE

Scene One

Lights up on a frozen street scene, rather like an L.S. Lowry painting. The picture remains still for a few moments, then bursts into life — noise everywhere as the people bustle about their business — all gradually leaving the stage.

BILL is left alone, holding an open book. He walks downstage and sits.

BILL: Now I perceive the reality of those days, and the ways that had us all. The streets and the mills and the houses — the people are now moving forms in colour and life before me. A true pity hurts me. I wonder if they have lost all thought of how it was. All material hurts and injustices will have left no mark on those natures. My memory is filled with those days and there is clarity everywhere. I walk in the cavern of my youth.

Closes the book slowly. A burst of noise and enter boys playing football with tin can. Others strolling, squatting, etc. Then enter, in a group, ERNIE, JIMMY, FELIX, SAMMY, SPADGER, BILL, PONGO.

SPADGER: Ideal place here, chaps. One man that end on 'nix-out' and one t'other end.
FELIX: Hang on, though, Spadge.
ERNIE: Scared, Felix?
FELIX: Is it likely I'm scared?

1

ERNIE: Well, if I were a betting man . . .

SPADGER: Okay Ernie. It's a smashing spot. Fine lookout. Play pitch 'n' toss here with no interference at all from the coppers, Felix. Who's on?

Several nod and grunt approval.

ERNIE: Not if Jimmy's 'nix-out'.

JIMMY: Why not?

ERNIE: Bloody false alarms, Jimmy, that's why.

JIMMY: It's confusing to tell with yon plain clothes tecs.

ERNIE: Aye, but you suspect every blighter, you do. Last time, know what? Jimmy shouts: 'Coppers!' and me and Pongo run — right, Pongo? Run round corner and into a brick closet to hide, and know what? We flung the door open, and had it shut behind us before we saw it was being used by an old fellow with a skull-cap on his head and his trousers round his ankles. Didn't know what to do.

JIMMY: Strange to say, I don't think he welcomed company, Ernie.

ERNIE: And all thanks to one of Jimmy's false alarms, as we later heard.

SPADGER: I've run right through somebody's house. The mother was 'siding' at the table. Frightened her to death, me at top speed nearly knocking her down with her hands full of pots. Straight through, front to back, and over the wall.

JIMMY: If Ernie Haddock thinks he can do it better, let him.

ERNIE: Don't weep, Jimmy. It aren't everything you can't do properly. No, Sammy and Pongo will keep watch, won't you, chaps?

PONGO: Aye, for starters.

ERNIE: Okay, Sam?

SAMMY: I don't mind.

ERNIE: No false alarms.

SPADGER: Who's pitching, then?

Game of pitch-and-toss begins, with SPADGER, ERNIE, JIMMY, FELIX. BILL *stands apart.*

SPADGER: Bill?
BILL: I've to get a haircut with the sixpence I've got.
SPADGER: Keep your hand on it, Bill.

Suddenly, PONGO *shouts out.*

PONGO: Lads! Quick!

The four players rush off.

It's Bob Thropper. *The* Bob Thropper.

The four return, as enter BOB THROPPER, *carrying a parcel.*

SAMMY: Bob Thropper the Centre Forward?
BOB: That's the name, lad. This is me.

The lads, except for SPADGER *and* BILL, *swarm around him.*

ERNIE: Hallo, sir. Carry your parcel, sir? On your way to the ground, are you?
BOB: Call me Bob, son. I'm Bob to the fans, not 'sir'.
ERNIE: Thanks sir. I will, Bob.
JIMMY: Terrific goal you scored against Barnsley, last match, Bob.
ERNIE: Care for a game with us now, sir? Bob?
BOB: Can't stop, lads.
ERNIE: Carry your parcel?
JIMMY: Where are you bound, Bob? Can we show you the way? Or assist you at all?
BOB: Bound for Dr. Paddy Bryce's surgery. I'm in line for a spot of massage. Shorts and towel in here.
ERNIE: Be honoured to show you the way to Paddy Bryce's, wouldn't we, chaps?

General agreement.

3

BOB: Well, I think I know . . .

ERNIE: No, see, there's a quick way for them as knows it, isn't there?

General 'yes'.

Let's show Bob, chaps. It's quite straightforward, by the shortest route, this way. . . .

They move instantaneously as two groups, in opposite directions. BOB THROPPER *strikes off, and they follow him.*

PONGO: Centre forward for the Wanderers, Spadge. You'd be advised to get to know him, you being the best school player in Bolton. He lives next door to my Auntie Florence. Coming?

SPADGER: You'll lose them, Pongo.

PONGO: Oh heck. (*He rushes off*)

BILL: Wanting to get a trial for his team, I thought, Spadge. You do, don't you?

SPADGER: If it's meant, no question but I will, Bill. Anyway, you have to remember one thing about Bob Thropper.

BILL: One thing? Don't be so close.

SPADGER: Buying and selling.

BILL: That a riddle?

SPADGER: When him and Bob Thropper was lads at school, the most promising goalie in the North was Sim Dalt, as now keeps Maggie Brunt's 'Beat the Goalie' stall in the Arcade, and at the fair.

BILL: I thought Sim Dalt was a bit simple in the head, Spadge.

SPADGER: Not with his goalkeeping hands he wasn't. They were lads together, and you're right: Sim was sent to Special School on account of being no kind of scholar. Bob Thropper evidently said — and just remember this — he didn't want no Special School dummies in the lads' team they played for then. 'Goalkeepers,' he said, 'I can buy 'em and sell 'em.'

BILL: Buy 'em and sell 'em? What did he mean?

SPADGER: I've no doubt he knew what he meant. Best get your haircut, Billy. (*Exit*)

Enter CHARLIE CRIDDLE.

CHARLIE: Bill, you've to stay. Me and Jimmy and Pongo have come by some luck.

Enter JIMMY *and* PONGO.

JIMMY: No luck in it. Hard sweat.

BILL: What doing?

PONGO: Carting loose coal into a coalshed.

CHARLIE: Got a tanner each. We're off to the fair to spend it. Are you set, Bill? Got any lolly?

BILL: Tanner for a haircut.

CHARLIE: Same as we've got each. I'll cut your hair. It was obviously pre-ordained to be. For sixpence, there's a lot you can do at the Fair.

Scene Two

Big scene change to fairground: Hoopla; Dartboards; Ringboards; Roll-a-Penny; Skittles; Coconut Shies; Sim Dalt's 'Beat the Goalie' stall; flashing lights, noise etc.

CHARLIE: Take it easy. Let's keep scouting round till we've found top value for money.

BILL: I'll stick with you, Charlie.

They circulate, then return to centre.

PONGO: Look at that hairy great coconut! I allus wanted to knock off a coconut — and I reckon that un'd drop with a touch.

CHARLIE: That's what you think.

JIMMY: I vote we all have a good feed on them hot peas. Just smell 'em. What you spend on your guts, my mam reckons, is never lost.

CHARLIE: Don't rush it, Jimmy.

PONGO: A coconut's the best bet. You might even knock two off, and they'd last for days.

CHARLIE: We didn't come by our money so easy, so let's use our discretion afore we part with it.

Drum-roll and cymbals. Enter behind in a spotlight a man dressed in silk shirt and riding breeches, carrying a silver-handled whip; and a woman carrying a revolver.

LADY: Ladies and gentlemen! Introducing Waldo, the greatest lion tamer of all time. Any moment now, he will enter the cage of Nero! Nero the Untameable! The African jungle lion that has killed four trainers — the largest lion in Europe — the fiercest in captivity. Waldo will positively enter his cage. Will he come out alive?

JIMMY: Hey — where are you off?

CHARLIE: Quick! Let's get in afore the crowd!

LADY: One small coin, ladies and gentlemen, sixpence only, brings you the greatest thrill of all time!

JIMMY: Keep still!

CHARLIE: Get your tanners ready. We can't afford to miss it!

JIMMY: No you don't. Black peas, a whacking great plateful for twopence, and finish off with roasted spuds.

PONGO: Big hairy coconuts!

HARRY and BASHER move off. CHARLIE and BILL approach the Lady.

CHARLIE: Half please. Bill?

BILL: Half please.

LADY: Half? Listen, you're going in for quarter tonight.

Two shillings the proper price. You don't expect to see a man eaten by a lion for threepence?

CHARLIE *waves to* JIMMY *and* PONGO, *who decline.*

BILL (*monologue to audience*): Inside the tent, we sat right down at the front. There were four people in there, and they looked at us pityingly. It seemed cold, after the bright lights outside. There was no sign of Waldo. After a long time, there was this beating on a drum, and the woman announcer came on and said:

LADY: During the act, ladies and gentlemen, there must be complete silence. One sound, and Waldo may never come out alive. His life is in your hands. Since no insurance company will insure Waldo's life, I ask any of you who can afford it to place an extra coin in the hat. Thank you.

CHARLIE/BILL: And on came Waldo. His face was all powdered, and there was a smell of stale beer off him. The curtain opened, and there was a cage. Lying in the nearest corner was a big lion. Less than a yard away from us it were. It blinked its eyes, and gave a big yawn. Waldo cracked his whip outside the cage, and Nero slowly got to his feet. Waldo went to the door, and sprang back when the lion came, which seemed to disturb the lion. As it moved away, Waldo opened the door and darted inside. He cracked the whip, and Nero loped wearily round the cage. After it he went, cracking the whip over his head. 'Silence!' called the woman. Nero skipped round the cage for about two minutes, then sank down to rest in the same corner. Waldo leapt to the door, opened it, and got out. Nero never moved. It looked at us again, blinked, sighed, and rested. The fiercest lion in captivity!

LADY: Ladies and gentlemen, that concludes the performance.

CHARLIE (*to* BILL): I can't believe it. (*to audience*) We

exchanged our last look with the lion as the curtain was drawn across the cage. We even clapped feebly with the others.

BILL *and* CHARLIE *clap feebly. As they are rising to go enter* ERNIE *and* SAMMY *cheering and throwing their hats in the air. The fairground noises return.*

CHARLIE: What chaps? What?

BILL: What's happened?

ERNIE: Where've you been? Tha's just missed the match o' the century, I'm not codding.

CHARLIE: I don't get you, Ernie.

SAMMY: Th'whole o' Bolton in years to come will be split between them as saw it and them as didn't.

CHARLIE: Flappin' Annie, what Sammy?

ERNIE: Who is — the idol of the Wanderers' crowd? Go on, who?

CHARLIE: Bob Thropper.

ERNIE: Right! Sam and me, we've just seen him.

BILL: Never!!

SAMMY: And have you heard it said as how his kicking power has broke many a goal net, knocked many a goalie senseless — ?

CHARLIE: Smashed a crossbar once I heard.

ERNIE: Right. Then listen to this. We've just seen Bob and some of the Wanderers' squad at Sim Dalt's 'Beat the Goalie' stall. 'Go on', one of the team says to Bob, 'You smash one in.' Bob's mates dive into their pockets for coppers when Sim calls out —

SAMMY: Like to make it pounds, not pence?

ERNIE: Eleven pound notes were flung down on the spot —

SAMMY: And Sim covered them with as many of his own.

ERNIE: Bob drew back, took one of his short runs, and let go one of his famous drives.

SAMMY: Sim was up like a flash, and brought it down with

all the style of a first-division goalie. He threw the ball back and said, 'Are you covering the twenty two quid?'

ERNIE: The money was covered in two minutes. 'What about waiting till sumdy nips off for your boots?' one of the team said. 'Boots!' says Bob, 'I could lick this loon in my bare feet.' And with that he took his second shot. It was good —

SAMMY: — but not good enough. Sim leapt and caught it on his chest.

ERNIE: 'Fetch me boots,' whispered Bob to one of his mates, 'an' I'll smash him to bits.'

SAMMY: The crowd went silent as he took the short run —

ERNIE: — and kicked. The ball flashed forward — it went like lightning. A knee-high shot. 'Goal!' somebody yelled!!

SAMMY: But a long thin figure whizzed through the air. There was a thud and the figure dropped to the ground. Nobody could be sure what happened — until Sim stood up. His face was white — but he had the ball clutched against his heart.

CHARLIE: I wish I'd seen it.

ERNIE: The crowd went mad. Volley after volley o' cheers.

Enter PONGO *and* JIMMY *following* SIM DALT.

PONGO: But won't your gaffer cut your wages now, Sim?

SIM: How's that then?

PONGO: Now you're the goalie Bob Thropper couldn't beat?

SIM: Was that who it was?

JIMMY: If Bob can't beat you, the rest of the world's no hopes.

SIM: Don't you worry lads. It's a good thing my gaffer can't pick me up and turn me upside down after a day's business. She'd have a shock at what might fall to earth. So long. (*He goes*)

ERNIE: We've not heard the last of this, lads.

SAMMY: Not by a long chalk.

PONGO (to BILL and CHARLIE): How was the lion
taming?

CHARLIE: Oh — champion. How were the hot peas?

PONGO: Lovely. Can you hear 'em churning about inside?

JIMMY: Not as good as my hairy coconut. Fair loaded wi'
milk. I knocked it off with the last ball. A right good
tanner's worth.

ERNIE: What lion?

CHARLIE: It were that exciting, as it took my breath away.

PONGO: Something did.

They all leave.

Scene Three

*Scene change to classroom, with rows of desks, a black-
board with the word 'Adverbs', and a teacher's desk
bearing an orange tree with seven oranges.*

CHARLIE: Who the 'eck have you been nudging ten minutes
past? After getting here early to finish, I'm trying to
finish.

BILL: Read what you've put, Chey. What's that?

CHARLIE: What's what?

BILL (reads): 'When the manks cam they fun Heerward
unconcon.'

CHARLIE: What art talking about? There are times when I
think tha must be going off thy nut.

BILL: Read that top line of thine, Crid. Just read it.

CHARLIE: I can see nowt wrong with it.

BILL: What's a *mank*?

CHARLIE: *Mank*? *Mank*? Tha means 'monk', you piecan.

BILL: Then why not write 'monk', Char?

CHARLIE: Oh, flapping Nora. Thanks Bill.

BILL: Then put *Hereward*, if it's Hereward the Wake.
Char, what's *fun*?

10

CHARLIE: *Fun*? Fun's *fun*. 'I *fun* a penny in t'street.'

BILL: Tha'll have four raps with Fat Ada's stick if tha doesn't change it. *Found*, you daft nut.

CHARLIE: Oh, holy mackerel, so it is, Bill. Quick, is there owt else?

BILL: Put 'e' on 'came'.

CHARLIE: Holy Moses, I were goin' at it that fast I didn't have time to cogitate. Go over it for us, Bill.

BILL (*reads*): 'He had thick golden hair growing down the back of his chest.'

CHARLIE: 'Chest.'

BILL: 'The back of his chest', Chey?

CHARLIE: Holy Mother, that would mean down his lungs, wouldn't it? An' me thinking I'd write the best composition of all time, that ud've been framed in letters of gold in the school hall, whereas I'd have got my bum smacked. Comes from not cogitatin', Bill. I'll remember thee in my will.

Pause as CHARLIE *corrects.* BILL *stares at plant.*

BILL: What I don't understand, Charlie, is how Fat Ada can love a plant in a pot, and not us.

CHARLIE: Orange plant! I reckon it's a potato plant off its beat.

BILL: There's oranges on it. Seven of 'em.

CHARLIE: It's her spy, you know.

BILL: Spy, Char?

CHARLIE: I swear, I crept in here one day when I wanted something from my desk, and there was Fat Ada whispering to that tree. I'm not coddin' — she were up against it, with one of them oranges as tha calls 'em all but in her kisser, and she was whispering away. An' you know what — the blessed tree were answerin' her back.

BILL: Geroff, Charlie.

CHARLIE: That tree tells her everything we say. I've watched her after she's been out of the room. She goes

11

to her little pet, and she knows everything what's happened. It's positively indecent.

BILL: If we could get it to talk for us, just think what it'd have against her — laying into us with that cane. And with her knuckles. Remember that time she cracked me round the ear for drawing a tulip as looked more like a cabbage? With that ring of 'ers, it near drew blood.

CHARLIE: It's witnessed cruelty without restraint to us, that plant.

Pause.
The silence is broken by the ringing of the bell. The class, which includes JIMMY, FELIX, SAMMY *and* PONGO, *enters. Some sit, but some gather around* CHARLIE *and* BILL.

ERNIE: Have you seen the front page of the *Despatch*? 'Waldo the Lion Tamer badly mauled by Lion.' Nero, fiercest in captivity — mauled the Great Waldo. Big letters, right across the page. I've told the lads we were all there when it happened.

PONGO: He's in a critical condition in the Infirmary, Char.

JIMMY: That lion'll be put down. Bound to.

PONGO: Is it true you was witnesses, Charlie?

Enter MISS TWINING *and* MAJOR PLATT, *Inspector of Schools.*

MISS TWINING: Boys!

They rush behind their desks.

Having heard the bell, and knowing we have a visitor this morning, boys, you surprise me. You know who our visitor is?

Murmurs of 'Yes miss'.

Major Platt, our Schools' Inspector, has come to spend

the morning, and I am standing in for Miss Skegham, who is unfortunately not in good health today.

MAJOR PLATT: Good morning, boys.

BOYS: Good morning, Major Platt.

MAJOR PLATT (*pointing at* CHARLIE): Young man. I hope you as an example don't make the habit of idling time away in over-loud conversation? Well?

CHARLIE: No, Major Platt.

MAJOR PLATT: Is there an explanation then for your all standing around gossiping like women, in whom it is but nature and thus excusable?

CHARLIE: No Major Platt.

JIMMY: Please, Major Platt, sir, it isn't Charlie Criddle's fault. We were asking him about seeing Waldo the Lion Tamer all but torn to bits last night. And William was there also.

MAJOR PLATT: Is that the person who was so severely mauled?

CHARLIE: It is, sir.

JIMMY: It just happens they were at the fairground performance last night when the Lion Tamer was mauled.

MAJOR PLATT: Then, Charlie Criddle, you'd better come in front and tell us all. Be seated boys. And be attentive.

CHARLIE *advances. He opens his mouth to begin, and then notices the boys, the teacher and the Inspector looking at him, and momentarily panics. He looks at* BILL *in alarm. Then he begins.*

CHARLIE: The lion . . . the fiercest in captivity . . . the lion was making furious deep-throated roars even before Waldo attempted to get into the cage. And when it caught sight of him in his blue silk shirt, it went into a fury. I was very close to the cage, and when its huge body hit the bars, it made the whole tent shudder. The roars were blood-curdling.

MAJOR PLATT: And . . .

CHARLIE: And very loud.

MAJOR PLATT: Good. Now the boy who was with you . . .
William . . .

CHARLIE: Sir! After three attempts to enter the cage, the
lady with the revolver . . . the pearl-handled revolver . . .
tried to dissuade the Great Waldo, but he refused to give
up, and I heard him say: 'The show must go on.'

MAJOR PLATT: Brave fellow! An example of fortitude.

CHARLIE: Then, by a ruse, he got Nero away from the
door, and the next moment he was inside. The iron door
slammed after him. He was now alone in the cage with
the African man-eating lion. A mighty roar rent the air
at that moment, and the big . . . the sizeable crowd
shuddered. Waldo attempted bravely to keep the lion
down with his whip — but it gave one spring. The next
moment, I saw his silk shirt fall to shreds on the floor.
But he was unhurt. He drove it into a corner. Again it
sprang. The woman darted to the bars with the revolver,
but I heard Waldo shout: 'Don't shoot!' His eye never
left that of the lion. For a long time it parried, trying to
knock the whip from his hand. Then at last it succeeded,
and again it sprang with an angry roar. Waldo fell to the
floor. But in a trice, he was clear. But he couldn't get
to the door of the cage. And he had lost his whip. The
lion seemed to be sizing him up. Then, just as it was
about to spring, he snatched a piece of . . . shirt, from
the floor, and waved it in front of his face. When it
sprang, he was already at the door. The blonde lady un-
fastened it. Just in the nick of time, he got out.

MAJOR: The African lion: proud, cruel, untameable . . .

CHARLIE: . . . Then I noticed a line of blood across his
brave back. The entire place trembled as the lion hit the
door. Waldo could scarcely stand up. I was right in the
front of the crowd. He gave a bow to the audience, and
then the lady helped him away. The audience clapped.

(*At this point,* CHARLIE *notices the word 'adverbs' on a blackboard.*) Madly. The lion snarled furiously. Then I went out modestly to meet my mates. One ate hot peas. The other clutched a hairy coconut.

Silence.

MAJOR PLATT: One day, my boy, you will make a true journalist. (*He takes a coin from his pocket and gives it to* CHARLIE) To encourage you to do which, I am pleased to reward you with this half-crown.

CHARLIE *and* BILL *are left as class and others disperse.* SAMMY *joins the astonished* CHARLIE.

SAMMY: The lion turned out to be the best sixpenn'orth after all, Char. (*He goes*)

BILL: Journalist, Chey? He wants to get himself a look at thy composition.

CHARLIE: Nay, Bill. Tha wouldn't wish to spoil the nice gentleman's day.

BILL: 'Modestly', Chey?

CHARLIE: Canst picture the real Nero in thy mind, Bill? The two old eyes, weary and worn. What agony it must have suffered to provoke the old jungle temper, eh? In fact, I had half a mind to confess the truth before the entire class. Only I felt a bit scared Major Platt might take his half-crown back. And I wouldn't wish to upset him, Bill.

*They go out together, laughing. Blackout.

Scene Four

When lights up, BILL *is discovered in the classroom, kneeling in punishment, and* CHARLIE *standing on a chair, hands on head. Silence.*

CHARLIE: Art game for a desperate measure, Bill?

*In the original production, the class sang an arrangement of the *Ave Maria* at this point.

15

BILL: Eh? Shout up.

CHARLIE: If I do, it'll hear. Art game for a desperate measure? Get your own back on Fat Ada?

BILL: How?

They both look at the orange tree.

BILL: She'd go stark raving mad. Anyway, what good would it do us?

CHARLIE: Tha doesn't look life square in the face, Bill. Tha's not got to think alone of thine own good. Justice has to be done. Let's say a Hail Mary together. We need her on our side.

They pray briefly, and then approach the plant.

CHARLIE: The wheel has come full circle, I am here. (*He picks up a pair of scissors from the table*) I think we ought to remove three apiece, Bill. Then we're in it up to equal culpitude. (CHARLIE *goes to touch an orange, but takes a woollen glove from his pocket. He puts the woollen glove on and snips an orange off quickly: as he snips the other two, the following:*) What is God, Bill?

BILL (*glancing up, worried*): You tell me, Charlie.

CHARLIE (*finishes cutting, stands back, admires, turns to* BILL): In my opinion, God is a supreme creamy caramel. (*Offers* BILL *the scissors over his arm*) Quick!

BILL *hesitates, then takes the scissors. He cuts one off.*

CHARLIE: Tha' cudgitates too much, Bill, till tha doesn't know where the hell tha' art. Has anyone ever told thee, th'art a very fussy lad?

BILL: Has anyone ever told thee, Charlie, th'art a damn fool?

CHARLIE: Frequently.

BILL: What about the one that'll be left on, Charlie?

CHARLIE: I was thinking we should leave it on as a reminder of her bereavement.

16

BILL (*snipping off the seventh*): It doesn't seem right, Charlie.

A noise offstage suddenly alerts them.

CHARLIE: Christ! There's someone coming! Listen! Happen they'll not be coming here. No time to get away.

They stuff glove, scissors and oranges in pockets, and CHARLIE *pulls* BILL *behind the desks.*

I have done the deed!

Sound of door opening. Nervously enter NORMAN TRIBLEY. *He goes to his desk, takes out a book, and nervously studies it. After a while:*

NORMAN: 'The square on the hypotenuse is equal . . . equal to the sum of the squares . . .' The sum of what squares? 'The square on the hypotenuse is equal . . .' What bloody squares? What's a bloody flaming sodding hypotenuse? Oh, mammy! Mammy! I can't do it! 'The square . . .' Oh mammy! Mammy! Mammy! I can't sodding sodding sodding do it do it do it! What shall I do, mammy?

Suddenly, NORMAN *grabs an inkwell, and drinks the contents dementedly. Inkwell to lips, he stops, eyes fixed on the orange tree. He drops the inkwell, whimpers, and makes for the door.* BILL *and* CHARLIE *stand.*

CHARLIE: Look at it. It favvers bloody naked.
BILL: It looks right daft without oranges.
CHARLIE: The gods are just.
BILL: It'll be the one o'clock buzzer soon. Come on. Thee go by the boilers. I'll go the other way. Meet you at the ironmonger's.
CHARLIE: Nick. Nick. Nick. We'll bury the organs it's lost deep in the brickfield Bill. No-one will know where.

They have both approached the orange tree reverentially, then rush off as the buzzer sounds noisily.

Scene Five

Street corner. Discovered: ROSIE BEARDSON, ELLA
  SHARLEY, PHYLLIS, *and one or two other girls. They
  have blankets, two poles, a housebrick, etc — equipment
  for erecting their 'field hospital'.* ELLA *holds the brick.*

ELLA: There's better places than this.

ROSIE: I wish you'd do less with your tongue and more
  with that housebrick.

ELLA: I was only saying . . .

ROSIE: Where?

ELLA: What?

ROSIE: These 'better places'. Name one.

ELLA: The gable end.

ROSIE: With all t'lads playing their eternal footer? Incon-
  siderate specimens. With them stampeding all round us,
  we'd get busted to bits. No, here'll do, thank you.

PHYLLIS: Perhaps t'lads are why she wants to move, Rosie.

ROSIE: Who encouraged thy contribution?

  Enter BILL, *thoughtful.* ROSIE *stares at him, trying
  to outstare him.*

ROSIE: We're perfect just here. Get plying that brick, Ella.

ELLA: Anything for the sake of peace, Rosie.

  ROSIE *holds the pole, whilst* ELLA *tries to drive it
  into the ground.*

ROSIE: You mawp! That were my finger! Ee, some folk
  do have mawping kids! Hi! Hi! You! (*She is calling*
  BILL) Will tha hit whilst I hold? (*He looks round fur-
  tively*) I said, wilt tha hit whilst I hold? Hey (*to* ELLA)
  give it 'im.

ELLA: I'll 'it it.

ROSIE: Don't be daft. It wants some strength. Give it 'im.

  ELLA *passes the brick abruptly to* BILL, *and it is
  dropped on* PHYLLIS's *toe. She wails.*

PHYLLIS: Oooooh, my toe!

ROSIE: See what you've done now, you mawp! She'll take her blanket home now.

ELLA: Never mind, Phyllis. You can be our first casualty. After all, we want a proper one.

ROSIE *picks up the brick and gives it to* BILL.

ROSIE: Go on, give it a clout.

BILL: What's it for?

ROSIE: It's our field hospital, and no remarks. (*She holds the pole; he hits it with the brick*) Good shot! Give it another!

ELLA: Let me knock t'other in.

ROSIE: Don't be daft. It needs a man on the job.

ELLA: A man or a sample?

BILL *looks at her abruptly.*

ROSIE: Don't tha be so cheeky, madam.

The other pole is knocked into the ground.

GIRL: Don't go yet. We need nails knocking into the wall.

ROSIE: Nails we can manage for ourselves. You can go now (*to* BILL).

They organize themselves to play hospitals, stretching a blanket between the poles and the wall as a cover, and using an old army top-coat as a bed, and a corrugated zinc washing-board as a stretcher. They fasten white cloths to their foreheads. BILL *watches* ELLA *from a distance. Enter* FELIX, SAMMY, HERBERT, ERNIE, SPADGER, PONGO, TOMMY, JIMMY, BASHER, *etc.* JIMMY *and* ERNIE *are arguing.*

JIMMY: We've had our share — our share and no more. Thy mam's allus the first in the queue at dinner-time.

ERNIE: Aye — but she gets her striker's free pea soup in a *jug.*

JIMMY: Art thou hinting, Ernie Haddock, about our mam supposed to have taken a chamberpot for soup?

ERNIE: I only said my mam gets ours in a jug.

JIMMY: That's a lie been spread about my mother. An' I only wish I could lay hands on him who started it.

FELIX: Talking about poes, did you hear about that lad at school as had to spell 'potato' and he spelt it 'tato', so the teacher says . . .

SPADGER: 'Where's your *po*, Willie?' she says, and Willie pipes up: '*Po*, miss? We aren't got one. We use a four-pound jam jar.'

FELIX: Why does tha allus have to chip in, Spadger?

ERNIE: Anyway, there's no such things as a *four*-pound jam jar. Jam jumps from two-pound to seven-pound.

SPADGER: Th'art thinking of pickles. 'Course, I wouldn't know for certain. We allus have our jam delivered in fourteen-pound jars of Shivers' best blackcurrant.

FELIX: Thy mam, Spadger Chadwick, buys twopenn'orth of loose jam in a saucer, plum an' apple, when you're lucky.

JIMMY: I'll let thee have it one of these fine days, Haddock.

ERNIE: Ah — shut your mouth, give your bum a chance.

JIMMY: Nowt but lies, start to finish.

SPADGER: Hush up, for pity's sake. Don't you know you're in danger of death for twenty four hours when you call a chap a liar? It's in the Bible.

JIMMY: He started it.

ERNIE: I never did.

SPADGER: Hush —

JIMMY: Tell Haddock then!

SPADGER: Are we sitting on sideset in our street or are we on t'Somme!!!?? Flapping Nora, a chap can only take so much. (*Pause*) Ahh, that's better — niff that quiet.

PONGO: Talking of wars. What about Charlie Criddle and Fat Ada today. Did he go to hospital?

BILL: He said he would.

SPADGER: What's Charlie Criddle done to upset her this time, Bill?

BILL: Saying the Beatitudes. Don't know what it is comes over him. It's not cheek — but you know what he's like. Suddenly, these words come out.

SAMMY: Fat Ada asks him to say the Beatitudes, see.

SPADGER: This is William's moment, thank you, Sammy. Continue, William. Uninterrupted.

BILL: And he comes out with all these daft speeches. 'Blessed are they that mourn, for after the funeral they shall be fed. Blessed are the meek, for they shall be un-meeked. Blessed are the merciful, for they shall be let off.'

SAMMY: Up squawks Fat Ada: 'Criddle, come out here! What a monstrous specimen! In all my years of teaching at this school, I've never come across anything or any-body like you, Criddle.' 'No miss?' asks Charlie. 'I were only putting in my own words.' 'Criddle, hold out your hand! Hold it out!' shrieks Ada. Chey holds it out, but as she raises the cane, he begins to curl his hand round from the front to the side, up near the shoulder. Ada notices this, and makes a dart with the cane to try and draw his hand out. Suddenly Chey shouts out: 'Oh my eye! Oh my eye!' Fat Ada says 'Up! Up!' and starts beating Charlie Criddle about the back with her cane. He lets out this howl, clutching his face: 'Oh my eye! You've hit me in the eye! You cruel woman!'

SPADGER: And had she?

PONGO: She says: 'Remove your filthy hand from your eye, and let me see!' One peep at it were enough. She sends Charlie Criddle with Billy down to the cloakroom to bathe his eye.

FELIX: What were it like?

BILL: A balloon. It were sore, an' all, Chey said. Nor it got no better when he bathed it. I told him to go off home to get his mam to take him to the Infirmary. It were all but shut up. Said it were crippling him.

21

FELIX: An eye like that can be very serious.

PONGO: Serve Fat Ada right if Chey's mam comes up. Her's as strong as a mule, the way she handles yon cotton bales.

FELIX: Her doesn't lift 'em herself. Her only works the blasted hoist.

PONGO: Well, somebody ought to assassinate Fat Ada one dark night.

BILL: It weren't her fault, according to Charlie.

HERBERT: How's that?

PONGO: It bloody was her fat fault. Flappin' Annie, I seen her do it.

BILL: Charlie says to me, down at t'washbasin: 'She never poked the cane into my eye. I did it myself.' He said she put the cane through his elbow, somehow, but it were him as shifted his elbow and it were him as sent the stick up into his eye. A sharp bit stung into it.

PONGO: Imagine her as anybody's mother, Spadger. Fat Ada. No, you can't. It wouldn't be natural.

Pause.

JIMMY: What was that from the Bible, Spadger — about being in danger of death?

SPADGER: Call somebody a liar, and you're in danger of death for twenty-four hours.

JIMMY: Is that right?

SPADGER: It's in the Bible.

ERNIE: Charlie Criddle's been in danger of death.

BILL: You can't die from a stick in the eye?

ERNIE: No — you and him and Waldo the Lion Tamer, last week, eh?

FELIX: Second time for Billy then — eh Bill?

BILL: What?

FELIX: Came close to supping enough arsenic to subdue a regiment.

BILL: Oh, aye — little Albert's baking.

JIMMY: Oh, not that one again.

FELIX: It were when we were all bound for fishing, eh, Sammy?

SAMMY: One o'clock on Saturday afternoon, and eleven of us setting out from our street. Suddenly, the woman at the end house, Mrs. Hoskey, bobbed her head out and shouted:

FELIX: 'Hy, will one of you boys go on an errand for me?' Boys, it's not worth it. She'll send you to the tripe shop for some trotters, to Clarke's for some toffees, to the paper shop for some love books, an' when you've worn your leather away, she'll give you a miserable bit of bread and jam.

SAMMY: A rotten jam butty! So Felix calls: 'Why don't you send Albert?' beckoning his thumb at little Mr. Hoskey, pegging out washing in the back street. She replied: 'He's busy!'

SAMMY: Then:

FELIX: 'Billy, love, you'll not see me stuck!'

BILL: She was a big fat woman with red hair, and I'd once heard said she could put the evil eye on you. I didn't want that happening just as I was going fishing. 'I'll not be long, lads!'

FELIX: And wasn't I right about the errand?

BILL: Except she had a quarter-ounce of snuff as well.

FELIX: I was certainly right about the jam butty. 'A nice little bit of Albert's baking,' she said, wrapping it up in paper to make it look a lot.

SAMMY: Albert cries, 'You can't give that to young Billy, Ada! I tell you it didn't rise properly!'

FELIX (as Ada): 'If you poke your nose into my business, I'll put you up the chimney. So help me.'

SAMMY: 'But it hasn't risen! Billy, don't eat it!'

BILL: His wife lets out one roar . . .

FELIX imitates roar; SAMMY recoils.

BILL: . . . and off I went with my jam butty. Albert's

23

advice was sound. I chewed it for a hundred yards or so, just to give it a chance. But then I marked one of those wide sewer grids along the street. (*He mimes spitting out the mouthful of bread, and stuffs the rest in his pocket.*)

FELIX: Meanwhile, at Pike's Lodge — the scene. Every inch of the muddy bank thronged with kids of all ages. Me, up to my shins in mud. All fishing away with all their might.

SAMMY *is joined by* PONGO *and* BASHER *to mime appropriately. They make sounds of 'perlop' of pin hitting water; 'perluff' of a writhing stickleback being pulled out.* BILLY *kicks up a sod of grass, paws at the soil, grabs a worm, unreels his line, and joins* FELIX.

FELIX: Beside me, a great big toffee-tin heaving with fish. (*He mimes drawing in two lines.*)

BILL: Seven! Four red doctors among 'em!

FELIX *looks sourly at his catch, and returns the two fish.*

BILL: Have you gone daft?

FELIX (*picking up the can*): There's nowt to it. I'm fed up to the back teeth. You throw in, and they're on before the worm hits the water. It aren't fishing. It's mass suicide. Even wenches are catching 'em.

He flings the rest of his catch back. SAMMY *joins them.* BILL *and he are amazed.*

BILL: I didn't feel so bad as Sammy, as I'd caught none yet.

SAMMY: What's on your mind, Felix?

FELIX: I want to do summat as needs a bit of doing. Such as catching a carp. A carp aren't like a stickleback. It don't bite.

SAMMY: What does it do?

FELIX: Sucks. A carp gives a suck to the bait to see if it likes it. The float does no more than tremble. Then tha strikes. That's what I call fishing.

BILL: Where can we catch carp, Felix?

FELIX: Our mill lodge.

SAMMY: Pratt an' Dysons'? Not a chance!

BILL: Why, the watchman?

SAMMY: No. The carp. Our old man has fished every lodge, lake an' canal in the British Isles, and he reckons there's no fish in this wide world wants as much catching as one of Pratt an' Dysons' carp. They're that pampered, they don't even suck.

BILL: What do they do?

SAMMY: Sniff. They just sniff the bait. And you gotta strike then.

FELIX: That sort of fishing, I'd say there was something to.

SAMMY: Aye, but nobody ever catches any.

FELIX: You don't have to tell me. I work there. Now surrounding Pratt an' Dysons' mill lodge is a very high fence with a barbed-wire top.

They walk along past an imaginary fence.

FELIX: The watchman has his tea from four to half-past. He's as deaf as a doornail an' can't see a yard in front of him, so don't worry.

BILL: Then I spotted a knot-hole in the wood. I peeped through. 'Oh — no use. There's one chap fishing.'

FELIX *shoves him aside and looks.*

FELIX: It's our managing director, Charlie Pratt. Come on, give me a cock-up, and see what he says.

They give him a leg-up. PONGO *mimes Mr. Pratt.*

'Llo, Mr. Pratt. I work in number seven room under Alec Ackers. Would it be all right if me and my mates had a quiet ten minutes with you?

PONGO (*as Mr. Pratt*): It will be quiet. I've been here since early morning and never a stir. But if you can get in, you're welcome to it. Don't say I gave you permission.

FELIX: Okay lads. (*He goes along the imaginary fence, tapping the boards*) There's a false un, if I can find it. Here it is.

Mime: removal of board; they climb in; FELIX *carefully replaces it. They pause a moment, unspeaking.*

SAMMY: It was as though we had entered some wonderful land, after all the mud and din of the Pike Lodge. It was beautifully quiet, everything spotless. The water was pale green, and the fat, lazy carp, some a lovely red and gold, were gliding about in the depths.

They begin to feel in their pockets for hooks and catgut.

SAMMY: Hey — what about bait?

FELIX: Crikey, these won't look at worms. We need some good dough.

PONGO (*as Mr. Pratt*): You can divide this bit up, lads. I've just about had enough.

A rush for the bait. BILL *is left without.*

FELIX: I hope we're not driving you away, Mr. Pratt?

PONGO (*as Mr. Pratt*): Ten hours, laddie, without a bite is enough, even for me.

He begins to pack away his fishing gear. The others are all by now fishing. BILL *has no bait.*

BILL: Suddenly, I felt the remnant of the jam butty in my pocket. (*He takes it out, and turns away from the others*) I couldn't separate the bread from the jam, so I put the lot in my hanky . . . (*He kneads it together, spitting in to it to make it doughy. He takes a little between finger and thumb, presses it on to the hook, settles, and casts in*)

BILL: Softly, I cast in. Suddenly my float disappeared.
What's up, I thought? Where's it gone? I half pulled out,
felt something there, and struck. Up came my line out
of the water. Wriggling and twittering at the end of it
was a lovely fat carp. I stared at it, flummoxed.

FELIX: Quick, somebody, where's can?

They gather behind BILL, *open-mouthed; he looks
round at them, and swings the line in, grasping the fish
in his left hand.*

FELIX: It was thick as a polony sausage, and full of life.

Amazed, BILL *unhooks the fish and holds it under
the water, as* FELIX *scrambles to fill the can with water.*

BILL: What's all the fuss about, man? Take your time.

*He mimes putting the fish in the can. They all look
in.* BILL *rolls another pellet of bait whilst they are en-
grossed in the fish and casts in.*

BILL (*as hook hits water*): Ping!

*They look up and return to fishing. As soon as they
sit,* BILL *jumps up, as* FELIX *calls:*

FELIX: You're in!

BILL *yanks it out; they gather again.*

BILL: Tak' it off, Felix.

Again, astonishment as they look on.

BILL: Though amazed, I had wits enough to stick the
hanky of bait down in my pocket. Little Albert's
baking, I thought — worth a fortune!

They now crowd close to BILL *to fish.* BILL *has three
bites, but loses all three. Finally, crowded out,* BILL
moves down the bank.

BILL: A pleading look from Mr. Pratt, and I slipped him a morsel of bait.

Mr. Pratt catches two fish, and BILL *several more; increasing puzzlement amongst the other boys.*

FELIX (*to* SAMMY): Sniff? They're biting like tiger sharks, tell your father. We've a round dozen. What about getting another can?

SAMMY: But just then the watchman showed up. 'You might be the boss during the week,' he said to Mr. Pratt, 'But I'm in charge over the weekend. I'm not having it.'

They gather their tackle. BILL *mimes holding the can.*

BILL: I was glad, for the strain was telling. I offered them all one apiece — keeping two for myself. The secret of the bait I didn't share, even turning down the hint of a bribe from Mr. Pratt.

PONGO, *as Mr. Pratt, comes and whispers to him.*

With carp fetching fourpence apiece, and gold ones a tanner, I reckoned I'd make a fortune over the season. All I had to do was play my cards right with little Albert and the watchman. (*Pause*) But then, as we turned the street corner . . .

They all regard the scene with surprise.

FELIX: I say chaps, what's everybody out for? What are they all chunnering about? Look Bill — the ambulance outside your door.

BILL: Out comes my mother, running to me, with a policeman beside her.

BASHER (*as* BILL's *mother*): Are you all right, love?

'She' embraces BILL.

BILL: Let go! 'Course I am.

PONGO (*as P.C.*): He'll be all right, ma. Are you the lad that had the jam butty given you by Mr. Hoskey at the end house at half-past one today?

BILL: Aye, I am.

PONGO (*as P.C.*): How do you feel?

BILL: Champion. Leastways I did.

PONGO (*as P.C.*): Come on, laddie. In the ambulance.

BILL: What for? Like this?

PONGO (*as P.C.*): Aye. There's no time to dress up. Keep calm, ma.

They mime ascending into ambulance, P.C. helping BILL's *mother; then mime sitting inside.*

FELIX: 'What's up?' I asked my mother. And she replied:

SAMMY (*as* FELIX's *mother*): Little Albert. Bashed Ada on the napper with a mallet.

FELIX: About time somebody did.

SAMMY: Only stunned her.

FELIX: What a pity.

SAMMY: That's why he gave himself up — to get safely out of her way.

P.C. closes ambulance door.

PONGO (*as P.C.*): When did you eat it, sonny?

BILL: Eat what?

PONGO (*as P.C.*): The jam butty.

Pause. Anxious looks.

BILL: I didn't.

PONGO (*as P.C.*): What? Stop! (*Jerk as ambulance stops*) What did you do with it?

BILL: The first grid I came to, I put it down.

BASHER: Oh, I'll warm you my lad, for giving us such a fright. (*'She' shakes him roughly*)

PONGO (*as P.C.*): You'll be all right, now, ma. I'll have him home with you in ten minutes. And I'll tell the prisoner to stop worrying about the lad. I'll tell him he never ate it.

BILL: What's all this fuss about a jam butty?

PONGO (*as P.C.*): It were dosed. Dosed heavy.

BILL: Whatever with?

PONGO (*as P.C.*): Arsenic! (BILL *steadies himself*) Enough to kill a regiment. It were all the top off the jam — where he'd planted it for her. And the bread itself were fair weighted with it. Don't breathe a word lad. It's God's mercy you're not stretched stone stiff in the morgue this very minute.

They descend from the ambulance.

FELIX: Hey, know what, Bill? Know what? The fish, every blooming one swimming round like mad, swelling up and dropping stone stiff dead.

BILL: 'Felix, forget it. There's nowt to it.' Leaving Felix staring flabbergasted at me, I staggered lightly up the street. I didn't know and I didn't care whether they'd fuss me at home or give me a right good hiding.

Exeunt all except HERBERT, ERNIE, BILL, ELLA, ROSIE, PHYLLIS *and* TWO GIRLS.

HERBERT: Coalpicking next week, chaps? Chatbent Pit's nearest.

ERNIE: I'm in. My mam's sick of having no hot water.

HERBERT: William? Spadger's coming.

BILL: I'm not sure . . .

HERBERT: Why not?

BILL: My dad's on strike . . . I don't know . . .

The boys are drifting off, ROSIE *pushes* ELLA *forward.*

HERBERT: Come on, Billy.

ELLA (*to* BILL): Rosie wants to know, will you play?

BILL: No. Sorry.

HERBERT *pats him on the shoulder, and goes.*

ELLA: She says it's only for once. We haven't had an officer, yet.

He reluctantly goes with her.

ROSIE: A wounded officer! Here, lay him down here on this bed. We'd better take his tempiture.

He allows himself to be laid down on the army coat.

BILL: Only this once.
ROSIE: That's a nasty wound in the forehead. We'd better get that bandaged. Sister, answer the telephone.

She 'bandages' him with an old shirt.

BILL: Hy — you're covering my eyes.
ROSIE: Quiet, please, captain. You're nearly blind. Any further wounds?

ELLA *feels his legs and listens to his heart.*

ELLA: No legs broken. Heart beating faintly.
BILL: I think I've to go.
ROSIE: Oh, but we can't discharge you in this state, captain. You've been at death's door, if only you knew it. Any more wounded on the battlefield?
PHYLLIS: I can't see any.
ROSIE: Go and look. You an' all. Don't you dare leave any soldiers to die of neglect.

ELLA *and* PHYLLIS *go out of tent.*

BILL: I think I'm cured now. I'm feeling a lot better.
ROSIE: Yay, yay. But first the lady doctor has to make sure you've no broken bones. Don't move, please. (*She feels his head, his ears, down the back of his neck, along his chest, his stomach, and then swiftly her fingers transfer to his ankles*) I think everything is sound. (*She*

31

feels slowly up his legs, and then puts her hand up under his trousers leg. A pause)

ELLA: I saw you, Rosie Beardson!

ROSIE: Eh? You saw what?

ELLA: Where you had your hand.

ROSIE: What are you hinting at, Ella Sharley, you dirty cat? I tell you I never did. I never did. And if you say I was, I'll thump your flaming lug for you.

ELLA: I saw. I saw you, Billy.

ROSIE: Did you hear that dirty little cat Ella Sharley? I'll tell my mother of her if she goes on like that.

BILL: No — don't do that!

ROSIE *packs up the equipment, with* PHYLLIS. ELLA *returns and chalks 'R feels up clothes with B' on the wall.*

ROSIE: Oh, look what that hussy's done. Don't worry, I'll wipe it out. It's not as though there was anything to be ashamed of.

BILL *goes.* ROSIE *alters the chalked message to read* 'ELLA *feels up clothes with* BILL' *and then goes; the 'field hospital' has gone.*

Scene Six

On the moors above Bolton.

BILL: She was at the meeting place. We didn't speak or go up to each other, just stood among the other people waiting for the trams. This was where I'd once seen a chap with no legs being lifted off. When the tram came she got on and went downstairs. I went on top, right up in the front where it was open. It seemed a long journey and I keep thinking of Ella below. We came to the terminus and I hurried down. Ella was already walking up the hill. As I followed her I looked back, down towards Bolton — lying like a huge saucer of smoke in the hollow. . . .

Lights up on ELLA *removing shoes and socks* — BILL *backs towards her continuing to look at the view.*

BILL: What you doing?

ELLA: Me feet're just crying out to have a touch o' this grass.

BILL: What if someone comes?

ELLA: It's back of beyond up here! Who's likely to come?

BILL: Farmer or summat.

ELLA (*stretching out legs*): Let 'im come, who cares?

Pause. With a few looks around BILL *approaches her and sits.*

ELLA: They say you can get a whiff of sea air from Blackpool up here some days.

BILL: Better than streets an' houses. (*Lies back; pause*) Hey — when you look at the sky it feels like you can see the world moving.

ELLA: Yeah.

BILL: Where did you tell your mam you were going?

ELLA: I said I had a girl to meet.

BILL: Will you get coppit, if you're home late?

ELLA: I don't care if I do. (*Pause*) I wish you had a sister and I was her and I lived in your house.

BILL (*sitting up*): Can I give you a kiss?

ELLA (*quickly*): Yes. (*Pause.* BILL *then moves to kiss her*) Suppose somebody comes?

BILL: Let's chance it.

They kiss quickly.

ELLA: When are we going to meet up again?

BILL: I'm going to Chatbent pit tomorrow, with the lads.

ELLA: Wish I could come.

BILL (*jumping up*): Shall we go back by Robert Murdoch Street?

ELLA: We've only just come!

BILL: I think it's going to rain. Come on. (BILL *strides off*)

ELLA (*standing up*): My shoes, Bill! (*She hobbles off after him*)

Scene Seven

The front of Bill's and Spadger's houses, which are adjacent. BILL, MICHAEL *and* SPADGER *appear at their bedroom windows. Nightsoilsmen are below them.*
Night. Sound of horse and cart.

SPADGER (*offstage, above*): Bill? Bill?

BILL (*offstage*): What?

SPADGER: Wake up Bill!

BILL: I am awake.

SPADGER: You've left your window open.

BILL: Doesn't matter.

SPADGER: Muckmisers, Bill. (*Pause*) I can hear them coming. (*Pause*) They'll be emptying the back privies, Bill. Any minute. Bill!

BILL: What?

SPADGER: Nightsoilsmen are here!

BILL (*appearing at window*): Flappin' Annie! Why didn't you tell us?

SPADGER (*also appearing*): Oh! Niff that pong!

BILL: It's all in my room now. How can I sleep? It'll wake our Michael up, an' all.

SPADGER: Whatever were you thinking of? Allus close window on a Thursday night — tha knows that!

BILL: I was wondering — when somebody touches you, can people sometimes see that their fingers have been there?

SPADGER: What are you fantasising now, Billy?

34

BILL: Sometimes, somebody touches you, and you can feel it hours after.

SPADGER: Sssh!

Enter two men with oil lamps, one whistling. BILL *and* SPADGER *watch.*

MAN 1: It's her cooking, though. Aren't like my mother's at all.

MAN 2: No. It'll be more like her mother's.

MAN 1: But if I say anything . . .

MAN 2: Don't say anything. Just praise it when it's good. It'll come right in time. Don't start criticising. It don't do with women. They're easily disheartened. Praise 'em and love 'em. It's best road in t'long run.

MAN 1: But . . .

MAN 2: I've told you, an' that's an end of it. I wish somebody had ha' told me when I first got wed.

They retreat upstage, and emerge with a big pail from privy offstage.

MAN 2: An' I never feel happy until my pockets are empty. I've allus been that way. Like they say, money seems to burn a hole in my pocket. I've got to get rid of it. Otherwise I'm never at peace.

MAN 1: I don't understand thee, Arthur.

MAN 2: I don't understand my blooming self.

They leave with pail.

SPADGER: Can you see the horse?

BILL: Aye, just. Two on 'em — big strapping shires. I think one's a bay.

Enter MAN 2 *with empty pail. Walks slowly, singing. After a moment,* SPADGER *joins in. The man stops and they sing.* MAN 2 *stops singing and returns pail offstage.* SPADGER *continues to sing.* MAN *returns and sings to conclusion, and then leaves.*

BILL: I know no-one round here who's a voice to match that, Spadge. I've never heard thee sing before.

SPADGER: I might say I know no-one who'd be up at this hour of the night watching shit merchants. Get thee to bed, you daft article. Go on!

Exit SPADGER. BILL *is joined by* MICHAEL, *his brother.*

BILL: Pong's my fault, Michael. I clean forgot nightsoilsmen.

MICHAEL: Couldn't sleep any road, Billy. I heard yon Spadger singing. He's a singing voice as nimble as his footballer's feet, that one.

BILL: One in a million.

Pause.

MICHAEL: The stink of Bolton, Bill.

BILL: Nay. It's not. Stink of shit.

MICHAEL: I'll remember it this road, leastways.

BILL: Remember?

MICHAEL: Promise of secrecy, Bill?

BILL: If tha wishes.

MICHAEL: I'm to elope, Bill. I've to leave Bolton, with yon Nancy. I've gotten her pregnant.

BILL: Does my mam know?

MICHAEL: Course she don't. There's neither mam and dad, nor Nan's family, can afford for us to be wed here. So you've to keep quiet till we've quit. Promise?

BILL: You can trust me.

MICHAEL: Cheer up. It's for best. It's no start in life here, I can give either Nan or the bab. Me with no job, nor any prospect of one. Strike seems never-ending into the bargain.

BILL: That'll leave just me and mam and dad.

MICHAEL: But for the three of you, it's a relief any road. I shan't expect to see Bolton again.

BILL: Where are you bound?

MICHAEL: Liverpool. We'll find a place in Liverpool. And work, Billy.

BILL: Mmm.

MICHAEL: I didn't want to go afore I'd told thee.

BILL: I'd rather come with you.

MICHAEL: When thy day comes, there won't be owt to hold thee in Bolton, eh?

Fade.

Scene Eight

The slagheaps of a coal pit; later the fields nearby and road home to Bolton.

   HERBERT *comes in with* BILL.

HERBERT: I've got thee a kitbag for thy coal, Bill.

   Enter around them SPADGER, ERNIE, SAMMY, JIMMY *and* TOMMY *who stand and contemplate the pithead, etc.*

HERBERT: There's the pit where thy dad works.

BILL: That — where the two wheels are?

HERBERT: That's it. Them's the winding wheels. Cage is under 'em. Down into the earth it goes.

BILL: Them tips — I never expected they'd be that high, Herbert.

HERBERT: Dark, steaming mountains where mountains never was intended.

ERNIE: I've heard it said, if tha takes milk to pit with thee, it's bloody butter by time tha gets down.

TOMMY: That'll be with the heat.

ERNIE: Nay, you mawp — the damned shaking.

TOMMY: Hot enough to turn milk up here, today.

SPADGER: Our old chap reckons it's worse nor Mesopotamia.

HERBERT: It's the heatwave from America.

SAMMY: I wish they'd blooming keep it.

ERNIE: There was a picture in t'paper this morning of a chap frying an egg on the sideset at Piccadilly Circus in London.

JIMMY: Oh aye — an' who had it?

ERNIE: Had what?

JIMMY: Bloody egg, you chump.

TOMMY: How the hell does he know?

JIMMY: Well, next time tha comes with a tale, come with a proper un. And all I can say is that a chap who ruins a good egg an' takes a photo of it just to tell folk it's hot when the flaming sun is all but setting 'em afire, deserves gelding.

HERBERT: Right. Let's get started.

JIMMY: Or shall we have our jackbit first?

HERBERT: We're never going to start eating *afore* work. Nay, it aren't come to that yet.

JIMMY: I only thought it would save time.

SPADGER: Jimmy, why dussent tell the truth — just for once? Just to give it an airing?

ERNIE: Seems contrary to be picking coal this weather.

SPADGER: Ask thy mother what's more contrary, Ernie — thee picking coal off tip, or her trying to cook and wash in cold water ever since the miners came out.

ERNIE: Don't talk to me about striking! I'm like Bill, me — us dad's pitman, so our mam daren't complain.

They have begun to search for coal to put in their various sacks. Mime the finding of coal. At points in the action, it will be possible for various of them to slip offstage to exchange their empty bags for full ones. HERBERT *approaches* BILL.

HERBERT: Nay, nay, that's not coal, lad. That's brass. So's that. And that. (*He empties* BILL's *sack.*) Bill, tha's not a gradely piece of coal in all that lot. Look, see that. That has only a surface of coal on it. That underneath is stone or brass. If tha took one of them home and thy mam put it on the fire, it'd blow up and smash your glass-backed dresser. Feel the weight. It's like lead. Now then, feel that piece. That's a lovely nut that is. Just the real weight. Feel it. This is not a heap of coal, lad. It's a heap of stuff, all sorts, spread out. Tha's got to pick, and scrape, for a black diamond. Keep thy eyes skinned. It'll take some finding. Here, I'll give thee that piece just for luck.

TOMMY *and* JIMMY *could by now have moved off-stage to collect full bags. Enter two slightly older boys.*

BOY 1: Hi, you lot. Eff off.

HERBERT: Who?

BOY 1: You an' your bloody mates. We don't want coppers round.

HERBERT: Language. Anyway, we're not going. We were here first. An' it's a free country.

BOY 2: You cheeky bloody monkey. (HERBERT *stands firm as he advances*) Art getting thyself off, afore I lay thee out?

HERBERT: If tha puts a finger on me, I'll par thy shins in. An' I'll raise such a din as'll bring every bobby for miles around.

ERNIE: Aye. An' I'll turn our dog as is just over there on thee, an' it'll chew thy cods off.

BOY 1: Pick away, lads. Just don't make so much noise.

SPADGER (*in a whisper*): It's a swealing, roasting, burning, parching hot day. In other words, warm. (*He sits, then leaps up and shouts*) Ooh! I've singed my arse!

Menacing looks from two boys as they go. Giggles from the rest, as SPADGER *tries to get through the following without making great noise.*

SPADGER: Hole in my trousers. I must've sat with that spot on a piece of hot slate. Who said they could smell roast pork? Fry an egg in the streets of London — what rot! I could roast a leg of lamb in this sun. Ooh, my backside! Can you smell it? Who said 'No more than usual'? I'm a right bloody comic, I am, and don't know it, Billy.

They both fall back laughing. HERBERT, SAMMY, *and* BILL *can have collected offstage sacks during the above.*

JIMMY: I vote we eat.
SPADGER: For once, Jimmy, I agree with thee.
HERBERT: I wonder where we can find a bit of shade?
TOMMY: We'd have to go across to yon trees o'er the field.
HERBERT: Aye, an' leave our bags. An' when we get back, they'd be empty. Not likely.

All but SAMMY *and* BILL *settle to eat their packed lunches.* SAMMY *drifts off.*

HERBERT (*passing a sandwich*): Here Bill.
BILL: Thanks very much, but I'm not hungry.
HERBERT: Get it down thee.
SPADGER: What, no tommy, Bill? Here, have a bit of mine. It's lovely stuff. Pig's dick an' lettuce.
TOMMY: If he wants another, he can have one of mine. Did you not get thy butties, Bill?
BILL: I've got some coppers.
HERBERT: Here . . .
BILL: I'll get some sweets. Ta. (*He moves off embarrassed.*)

Enter SAMMY *at a run.*

SAMMY: I just missed it.
HERBERT: Tha's missed thy wind.
SPADGER: Nay, he's not. He's more nor he can get shut of in time.
TOMMY: Missed what, Sam?
SAMMY: Butterfly.

ERNIE: Now, Sam, did tha strike?

SAMMY: Of course I did. Well, I did an' I didn't.

ERNIE: How the flapping heck does tha expect to catch a butterfly without striking?

SAMMY: I were just about to strike when I could see I might crush it. And I had it cornered a bit later but I were worried about batting all the pollen off its wings. They say a butter' dies if tha bats pollen off its wings. I woulda copped it. I would — only I were frightened of hurting it.

ERNIE: Tha means tha were frightened of it turning on thee. Not as I blame thee, Sam, for a butter' can be very nasty when it turns. I once got attacked by a Red Admiral — Christ, what a din they make when they bat their wings!

SAMMY *wanders off.*

ERNIE: He's got a brick loose up here has old Sam. He'd sooner have a butterfly than a gold watch. But I've never known him to catch one yet. He's allus frightened of striking.

TOMMY: There's one thing about Sam — he can lick any runner I've ever seen.

ERNIE: He were dropped out of the Olympic Games on account there wasn't enough room to pin a medal across his chest!

JIMMY: If somebody were to offer thee five bob for all thy coal, Herbert, would tha take it?

HERBERT: Not likely. I'm taking it home. I wouldn't sell it for ten bob.

ERNIE: For two bob, a sup o' cold water, I'd sell my coal, myself, an' all our sodding family.

HERBERT: That's not in the spirit of the trip, is it, Spadger?

SPADGER: Nay, Herbert. Don't worry. I'll not sell. None of us will — right?

ERNIE: Look out! Snigs!
JIMMY: Where?
ERNIE: Look — two of 'em.

Scramble to pick up bags of coal — 'Gimme a lift!'
'Gimme one!' etc; but HERBERT *stands firm.* SAMMY
only manages to hoist sack to shoulders.

TOMMY: Let's make a dash for it. Come on, Billy!
BILL: Herbert!
HERBERT: I'm not seeing good work go to waste.

SPADGER *and* JIMMY *have gone, leaving their bags.*
SAMMY *struggles with his.* BILL, HERBERT *and*
TOMMY *are left onstage. Enter two* POLICEMEN.

P.C. 1: What's the game, eh?
HERBERT: We've been picking coal to take home for
the fire.
P.C. 1: Fire, this weather?
HERBERT: Tha knows very well tha can't do a gradely
week's washing without a boiler fire.
P.C. 1: And tha knows tha's liable for trespassing, as well
as for stealing. Strike or no strike, this coal is the owner's
property, and can't be removed by any soul who can't
do the week's wash. So you'd better empty yon sacks.

No move from HERBERT.

P.C. 2: Come on, Harry.
P.C. 1: By gum, this is a stubborn little monkey.
HERBERT: How are they coping with wash in thy house,
then?
P.C. 2: Leave it, Harry.
P.C. 1: Do you smoke lad?
HERBERT: When I have some.

P.C. 1 *takes out a packet of cigarettes and gives one*
to HERBERT.

P.C. 1: Your two mates haven't much to say for themselves.

HERBERT: They're like me; they've too much on their minds for gabbing.

P.C. 1: Light? Now do get off afore the Inspector comes.

TOMMY: Aye, we will, officer.

HERBERT: Thank you very much, sir.

The policemen go. HERBERT *waves. Re-enter the other three.*

JIMMY: What did he say?

HERBERT: They said you were a bunch of windybags.

SPADGER: Spadger, you cowardly caitiff. Salute your officer at once. (*He salutes* HERBERT.) Time to move off, sir. Come on, Billy. Death or glory.

They pick up sacks and move off, sprightly at first, but slowing down as weariness increases.

TOMMY: I vote we stop an' ask for a drink of water.

JIMMY: Aye, happen somewhere they'll give us something to eat, an' all.

ERNIE: Let's call at that big house on the left.

HERBERT: Nay, not there. That's Squire Kershaw's house.

ERNIE: Herbert's windy of calling on the Squire.

HERBERT: I'm not windy. And I'm not a bladderhead. You can all go against me, and I'll call with you, and you'll see what you'll get.

ERNIE: Notice them flowers, and them lace curtains, Spadge?

TOMMY: Let's go back.

SAMMY: Aye, we'd better.

SPADGER *looks at* HERBERT.

HERBERT: We've come so far, we might as well go the whole way.

A female voice from inside:

43

LADY 1: What do you want?

HERBERT: Well, lady, we wanted a drink of water, if it's all right with you, please.

LADY 1: It most certainly is not all right. Get out! Off with you! Away, you filthy rascals!

HERBERT (*standing his ground as the others creep away*): There's no need to be rude, missis. A civil question deserves a civil answer. We're human, you know, same as you and yours. (*to others*) That's no squire's wife, I'll warrant.

SPADGER: It's our country as much as it's hers.

JIMMY: What about that little cottage across there?

HERBERT: Aye. We're nobbut four hundred yards from Coal Lane End. A mouthful of water there and we'd make it.

As they approach, a lady emerges. Her accent is local.

LADY 2: Sit down in the shade, lads, and I'll bring you some tea out. That's what you want.

HERBERT: We might do as much for you one day.

The lady goes for tea. They sit.

ERNIE: Aye, you never know your luck in this world.

HERBERT: Here, Sam — get a handful of coal out of each bag, an' bring it in thy cap.

Lady returns, with tea and cake. General thanks.

LADY 2: It'd be a poor day when a person couldn't help them as are helping their families.

SPADGER: We're not selling the coal. It's going to our mothers.

LADY 2: Of course it is, son.

HERBERT: If all the world was like you, it'd be a happier place to live in, missis.

She goes.

ERNIE: Same as my mam says. It's the poor as helps the poor.

SPADGER: Poor? Talk for thyself.

ERNIE: Taking it all round, tha couldn't call us rich.

SPADGER: Aye, an' we're not poor.

HERBERT: We, are what you would call the *middle* class.

TOMMY: Middle of what?

HERBERT: We're in the middle, between the top and bottom. You've got royalty and the aristocracy right at the top, and at their tails, all them with money. Down at the bottom, you've got the poor. We're what they call the middle class.

SAMMY: Am I middle class?

ERNIE: Thee, th'art in a class of thy own. Th'art a bloody ape as has lost its way.

SAMMY: Suits me.

ERNIE: An' who do you call the poor?

HERBERT: Them as *are* poor. Folk as never know where the next meal's coming from. Folk as can't keep body and soul together.

TOMMY: Abroad, my old chap reckons there's millions live on a handful of rice a day.

ERNIE: What — between the lot of 'em — or one apiece?

TOMMY: One apiece.

JIMMY: I like rice pudding, I do.

HERBERT: Pudding! They never see a drop of milk from one year's end to another. They die off like flies. An' in this country, there's slums where poor little kids crawl about covered with sores, crying their hearts out for a jam butty.

TOMMY: We're living in a fools' paradise, and don't know it.

ERNIE: We're living in a fools' summat.

SPADGER: Fancy him trying to put us in the lower class. An' *we've* got a concertina!

Enter most of the rest of the company as coalpickers 'of the poorer kind', streaming home, resting, some with handcarts and trolleys; one boy pulling a bag on a roller-skate.

HERBERT: Now, lads, can we do Coal Lane End in one go?

The gang joins the stream of coalpickers. TOMMY *tries to rest; a householder emerges.*

HOUSEHOLDER: Where d'you think you are? This isn't a public rest hall. Shift your sack and yourself off my doorstep, double quick!

BILL (*downstage*): I watched the ever-moving flow of people and coal. Wheels, wheels, wheels, I thought. Everything moves on wheels. Many of the pickers who were carrying their bags attempted to board trams with them, but they were turned away. Some, however, did force their way on, and couldn't be got off. One cheery driver called out: 'Room for a bag or two here in front', and there was such a rush that he couldn't get to the controls to drive away, for an enormous pile of bags suddenly rose up in front. (*He sits*) I had at last no interest in anything. The wheels and the bags moved by. The feeling of rest was beautiful. It all felt nice and light and floating. I didn't want to be disturbed. When a thought of my mother and home came up, I had to shut it out, because it made me feel like crying. Someone gave me a lime-drop.

HERBERT *does so. The crowd gradually disperses.*

ERNIE: I like pies well done. I won't half have a feed when I get home.

SPADGER: Tha'll have pea soup. Same as us all. An' what soup! One pea to a quart of water, an' he takes it out half-way through so it won't be too strong.

HERBERT: A chap can enjoy a crust of bread if it's paid for.

JIMMY: Aye, Herbert. You can't eat in peace unless you can keep the house-door open.

ERNIE: I can. An' give me a nice juicy bit of roast pork on the strap than all your bloody crusts as was paid for. And I don't care whether the bloody door's open, shut or missing.

WOMAN: Going far?

JIMMY: Not too far.

WOMAN: I could do wi' a bit of coal for my oven. Are you selling?

HERBERT: Sorry missis. We're taking it home.

ERNIE: Missis. You can have mine.

WOMAN: Is it good stuff?

ERNIE: Best trencherbone nuts. It'll do your pies in half the time.

WOMAN: How much for that bag?

ERNIE: Two-and-a-tanner, missis. An' I've humped it all the way from Chatbent Colliery.

WOMAN: Say two bob.

ERNIE: You're on. Shall I carry it in the front?

HERBERT: Nay, nay, Ernie. Tha can't sell up. What will thy mam think?

ERNIE: She'll be satisfied if I give her a bob out of it.

HERBERT: But if tha wants to sell thy coal, sell it to Granny Hayes. She's short of it.

ERNIE: And do you think she'll thank me for carrying it that extra half-mile? Out of the way, Herbert. I'm selling while I've got a buyer. (*He goes*)

JIMMY: It's all right for thee, Herbert. You've regular money coming in.

HERBERT: Only my sister's.

ERNIE *returns, and hustles* JIMMY *and* TOMMY *in.*

ERNIE: Come on, lads. She'll have yours too.

HERBERT: Not mine.

ERNIE: You'll get no credit for it when you get home.

Get what you can when you can. That's my motto.

He, JIMMY *and* TOMMY *go.* HERBERT, *disappointed, leaves with* SAMMY.

HERBERT (*going*): So long, Billy. So long, chum.

BILL *wearily drags himself to his feet and leaves. The following conversation is offstage.*

BILL: Hallo father.
FATHER: That you, Billy? What kind of bloody sight are you, in all that filth and dirt.
BILL: I brought coal home for mother.
FATHER: Coal — from where?
BILL: Chatbent Pit.
FATHER: What? You picked it? Took coal from the bloody swines of pit-owners? You'd break the strike? You, you bloody renegade! Give me that bag!

The coal is hurled onstage, into a pool of light; then blackout.

Scene Nine

In front of the gable end.
Light comes up on BILL. *Enter* CHARLIE CRIDDLE, *one side of his head bandaged.*

CHARLIE: Forget thy friends, Bill?
BILL: Charlie!
CHARLIE: How's Fat Ada, Billy?
BILL: Not much changed. Th'art out of hospital, then?
CHARLIE: At last. I'm forbidden school, though.
BILL: Th'art lucky, then.
CHARLIE: What else is a chap to do?
BILL: Plenty.

Pause.

CHARLIE: Has my mam told thee — they've nicked it out? (*Pause*) An' I'm to have an artificial eye. The best money can buy, says my mam.

BILL: How 'the best'?

CHARLIE: It all festered up, an' the eye doctor said it'd be best to have it out in case it got hold of t'other. I wanted a patch, but my mam said I couldn't go round looking like a pirate. 'Artificial eye, the best that money can buy!' I said, 'You're a poet, mam!' He is a fool, an' doesn't know it, who makes himself a craphouse poet. I don't want it favverin' a real eye. Give folk a shock when it ain't. I were reckoning it up, Bill. I know four lads wi' only one eye, an' three grown-ups, one a woman. How many does tha know, Bill?

BILL: I know two lads.

CHARLIE: To talk to?

BILL: One to talk to — one not. Three — did I say two? No, three.

CHARLIE: I've been wondering which eye you wink with when you've a glass un. If you wink with your proper eye, it means you go blind for a time, an' you can't see who you're winking at.

BILL: I know a blind chap, Chey, who can hammer in the dark.

CHARLIE: I were cogitating last night, Bill, about dark an' that. Say you get a field at night covered in darkness — is that just black daylight? I were cogitatin' on an invention called *black* electricity, or *black* gas. Instead of folks havin' to buy blinds, and curtains, and stuff, they just press a button, and there's a bulb or a mantle what comes on full blast with *black* light. Fills every corner of the room with darkness. They could have two switches — white for lighting up, and black for darking up.

BILL: It'd want thinking, Chey.

CHARLIE: Well, think it out. Han they said prayers for me at school?

BILL: They should've. Anyway, we'll be going up to Mr. Denning's class for our last few weeks, soon.

CHARLIE: I've told you before, an' I'll tell you again — it were my fault an' not hers. She had nowt to do with it, except she were holding the cane. Fair's fair. Come to think of it, Bill, chap as made the cane were one of the first causes, barring him as planted it. That's the rotter we want to get at. How's the orange tree?

BILL: It'll never lift its head again. Char, I can't agree it's none of her fault. She's to blame, not bloke as made the stick! She's got away with it. Why hast let her?

Pause.

CHARLIE: I wonder will any oranges grow where I planted 'em? They'd be ours, and Fat Ada's by right.

BILL: There's no right, and fair's not fair, Chey. (*no reply*) How is it?

CHARLIE: What?

BILL: Your eye.

CHARLIE: Which eye?

BILL: The one you've had out.

CHARLIE: A daft question, that, Billy. How do I know? I'll bet t'cat's had it by this.

BILL: Where it was.

CHARLIE: Socket. Feels like a factory lodge.

BILL: What, wet?

CHARLIE: Is it heck as wet! It's that flapping big. Her's a damn good teacher, tha knows, Bill.

BILL: Tha calls Fat Ada a good teacher, Chey? After . . .

CHARLIE: My dad were in her class. Course, she were only young then, but she clouted his lug more than once. He used to say to me when he was on leave: 'Tha'll never learn owt, lad, till old Fat Ada gets hold of thee.' He got killed in the war, tha knows. He went through it in the trenches without getting so much as a scratch, an' got himself killed in the last fortnight.

BILL: God rest his soul.

CHARLIE: Thanks. He allus swore by Fat Ada.

BILL: She were responsible, Chey.

CHARLIE: Take these who go to Proddy schools — they never get a real good tanning like we do. And look at 'em — just look at 'em. They'd think the eight beatitudes were a bloody football team. As for things like affinity, consanguinity, and spiritual relationship, they wouldn't know either one of them from a black pudding. Don't say owt against Fat Ada to me.

BILL: But what is consanguinity, Charlie?

CHARLIE: Tha doesn't know what consanguinity is?

BILL: I did know. But I've forgotten.

CHARLIE: Come to that, so have I. Let's away to the woods, Billy. Allez. Touchsweet.

Fade.

ACT TWO

Scene Ten

A back ginnel; then Mr Bidwell's office at the locomotive works.

> SPADGER *leads* BILL *on quickly.* BILL *is fed-up — hands in pockets, head bowed.* SPADGER *is, as ever, spry and cheerful. He places* BILL *centre stage and begins.*

SPADGER: The first thing I have to tell you is that Mr. Bidwell will not give a job to any lad in his loco shed that has been spoken for. He's dead against any kind of influence.

BILL: Don't want to work in the loco sheds. You have to be about fifty before they let you look at a train let alone drive one.

SPADGER (*firmly*): As I were saying, Mr. Bidwell believes that any lad what works for him should be able to speak up for himself. So thee'll have to go there and ask for a job thyself.

BILL (*panic*): I thought you knew somebody who was going to speak for me.

SPADGER: I do, but I told you, Mr. Bidwell don't hold wi' influence. Now I'll tell you the first thing Mr. Bidwell cannot bear the sight of.

BILL: What's that?

SPADGER: He can't bear the sight of a lad with his hands in his pockets.

BILL *pulls his hands quickly out of his pockets.*

SPADGER: Mr. Bidwell likes to see a lad with his shoulders well back. . . . (*pushing* BILL's *shoulders back in a way which is obviously painful*) An' he likes to see 'em stand as straight an' erect as a Coldstream Guardsman — head back and chin in. . . .

    BILL *tries to pull his chin in, pull his head back and stick out his chest all at the same time.* SPADGER *pauses and looks on with pity.*

SPADGER: Mr. Bidwell doesn't allow any mumblin' or mee-mawin', such as 'D-d-do y-y-you w-w-want any l-lads, Mister?' Anything like that drives him mad. You've got to speak in a loud, clear voice — 'I've come for a job, sir!' An' be sure to say the 'Sir!' as though you meant it. Now to come to the main point. There is one thing that Mister Bidwell must have.

BILL (*weakly*): What's that?

SPADGER: A real good smile!

BILL: How do you mean?

SPADGER: I mean — he cannot bear the sight of a miserable lad. Right. I think we'd better have a rehearsal. You see, Bill, your whole future depends on that smile. Do you follow me — the job you're doing in forty years from today will depend on the smile you give to Mr. Bidwell.

BILL (*terror clouds* BILL's *face for a moment — quickly replaced by resignation as he sees* SPADGER's *determination*): What do you want me to do?

SPADGER: Go over there.

BILL (*goes upstage and turns*): What now?

SPADGER: Imagine you're a lad out of work.

BILL: That won't be hard.

SPADGER: Then come over here — imagine that I am Mr. Bidwell and you've come to ask me for a job. Keep in mind the smile.

SPADGER *turns his back on* BILL, *assumes a fierce expression and stands legs apart, hands on hips. Meanwhile* BILL *struggles to stand up straight, pull head back, chin in, hands stiff by his sides. Still for a moment then forces a very grim and weak smile to appear on his face.*

SPADGER: Come on then. Let's have a look at you.

BILL *moves awkwardly across stage — right arm swinging with right leg. As he reaches* SPADGER, SPADGER *turns and looks. A pause whilst he tries to conjure up some comment —* BILL *is grotesque.*

SPADGER: Can't you show your teeth a bit more?

BILL *bares teeth — more like a rabid dog than ever.*

SPADGER: I'll tell you what — keep practising over the weekend. Do it like this — (SPADGER *walks confidently about with a huge smile on his face shouting out 'Good morning, sir! Good morning sir!'*) You get in there — first thing Monday morning — and we'll meet up at tea time (*leaves smiling and shouting 'Good morning, sir! Good morning my dear sir!'*)

BILL *is alone — comes downstage and begins trying out some smiles. Enter behind him a couple of lads deep in conversation — they stop and lean on wall still deep in their talk.*

BILL (*having found a smile suddenly bursts out*): Good morning sir!

The lads look up and round to see who he's talking to.

BILL: I've come to see you about a job. Please do not shake your head, sir, for I will not take no for an answer. I don't want anyone to speak for me — I'll speak for myself. (*Rolls up sleeves*) Lead me to your shed, sir. Honest labour bears a lovely face is what I say. The keystone of my philosophy, sir!! (*Smiles, leaves with confidence.*)

Enter a man in overalls looking at a large blueprint — which he begins to roll up. A knock off stage.

MAN: Come in.

Enter BILL *at the march with large smile.*

BILL: Good morning, sir!

MAN: Morning laddie.

BILL: I've come for a job sir.

MAN (*rolling up blueprint quickly*): Oh aye — then you'll have to —

BILL: I don't care how low I start, sir. I'll soon work my way up. And what's more I can start work this very minute.

MAN (*smiling*): Can you now?

BILL: I've studied your career structure, sir. It's a great future with the railways. Dirt wiper, greaser, oiler and greaser, fireman, culminating in the prince among workers, the engine driver.

MAN: Prince — you're right there.

BILL: Now on what job, sir, would you like me to start?

MAN: (*smile replaced by frown*): I'm not sure. It's not for me to say, not rightly.

BILL: Oh, but it is. I'll do anything you tell me.

MAN (*shaking head*): I think it'd be better if you were to wait and see Mr. Bidwell.

BILL: M-m-mister who?

MAN: Mr. Bidwell (*reaching off stage and producing a broom*) I'm only the sweeper up.

BILL *slumps — his hands go into his trouser pockets.*

MAN: Aye up. Here's Mr. Bidwell now.

Enter MR. BIDWELL — *a bulldog of a man.*

MR. BIDWELL: What do you want?

MAN *slides to one side.*

BILL: D-d-do y-y-you w-want any lads, mister?
MR. BIDWELL: Eh? What? Speak up. I can't hear a word
you say.
BILL: Do you want any lads?
MR. BIDWELL: Lads! Lads! No! I don't want any lads.
Certainly not a specimen like you! I wouldn't take
you on at any cost! (*Brushes past* BILL *as if to leave*)
BILL (*suddenly angry; hands coming out of pockets*): No,
an' I jolly well wouldn't take you on at any cost.

MR. BIDWELL *turns and is speechless.* BILL *puts
his hands back into his pockets, sticks chest out and
swaggers to leave. As he passes* MAN *he says:*

BILL: S'long mate, I wouldn't have your job at any price.

He leaves. MAN *looks at* MR. BIDWELL *expecting
the explosion. Blackout.*

Scene Eleven

In front of the gable end.
Enter BILL — *sits on floor — looks about then takes a
doorstep butty out of his pocket and begins to eat.*
ERNIE HADDOCK *and* SPADGER *enter together.*

ERNIE: Wut game, eh? Wut game art on, Bill?
BILL: Howgo chaps.
SPADGER: Thought you'd be on t'footplate of Flying
Scotchman by this.
BILL: Eh?
SPADGER: Winging your way through England's green
and pleasant land.

BILL: I'm a lost cause, Spadge.

ERNIE: Spadge said you was working up Loco sheds.

BILL: No.

SPADGER: Take therefore no thought for the morrow.

ERNIE: What happened?

SPADGER: Tha's in the trough of despond, Bill, me old top, sat here on this side set; an' wi' out our timely intervention who knows what'd become of you. He showed your britches bottom his clog-toe did he?

ERNIE: Who did, Spadge?

SPADGER: Mr. Bidwell.

BILL: I'm glad really. Reckon I'll go down John Kershaw's, see if they'll take me on in the weaving shed.

ERNIE: Ha! Wi' all them wenches?

BILL: They're not wenches. They're old women.

ERNIE: Not all.

SPADGER: Come in't snuffy wi' me.

BILL: Can't Spadge. Me mum and dad'd go mad if I worked in the dirty snuffy.

Enter MAN *who was the sweeper up in Mr. Bidwell's office.*

MAN: Eh, young 'un. Eh — thee!

BILL: Flappin' Nora; Bidwell's sent yon chap to lay me out, I know it.

ERNIE: What've you done?

SPADGER: He'll not touch you, Bill.

MAN: Eh, laddie, I've scoured every street and back ginnel in Bolton for thee.

ERNIE: Keep me out of it, Spadger.

SPADGER: Hold you hush, Ernie. (*to* MAN) Now then, what does Mr. Bidwell want wi' my mate?

MAN: He wants him to start work at the loco shed to-morrow morning.

BILL: You're codding!

MAN: It's a fact. He liked the way you spoke up to him.

He felt you were an honest lad, and if there's one thing
he admires, it's honesty.

SPADGER: Wut say, Bill, eh?

BILL: Thanks mister, but no. Not now. I've set my heart
on the weaving shed.

MAN: It's a great future.

BILL: I know.

MAN (*smiles*): I'll tell him then.

BILL: Thanks for your trouble.

MAN: It's nothing. Ha! Can't say I blame you. He's a
funny chap is Mr. Bidwell. (*Exit*)

SPADGER: One door closes — another opens.

Fade lights; ERNIE *and* SPADGER *exit.* BILL *remains. The deafening noise of a weaving shed.*

Scene Twelve

*A weaving shed. The effect of the weaving shed must
be created by the noise and by lighting — some sort
of effect like faded daylight falling in bars through
windows. Probably the only set required would be
a work bench backed by spare bobbins and tools plus
a stool. There should also be an enamel jug and mug
with water.*

*   BILL is left in a central light from the end of the last
scene. Fade noise to allow his voice.*

BILL: Hundreds of looms palpitating under the vast low
ceiling of the shed. And under the coarse glare of the
gaslight I could see the weavers — all women — long
lines of them, young and old.

*   HETTY appears at his shoulder suddenly out of the
darkness.*

HETTY: What do you want, luv?

BILL: Eh? (*he turns startled*) Eh? Eh? Sorry I want —

Although he's shouted these last words the woman can't hear him. She puts her hand on his shoulder.

HETTY (*leaning towards his ear*): Who?

BILL: Mister Hambull. Th' overlooker.

HETTY (*nodding*): That's Eddie (*indicates a man who sits asleep at workbench*)

BILL: Ta. Ta very much.

    HETTY *disappears quickly into the darkness as* BILL *moves slowly towards the sleeping figure.*
    The man is sound asleep with a large spanner gripped in his hand. It is obvious that, in all the din, BILL *is a bit stuck as to how to wake* HAMBULL. *He goes to touch him but changes his mind. Worried* BILL *clears his throat. At this the man leaps to his feet.*

HAMBULL: Urrroww . . ! Wut game, eh? eh? Wut game art up to? Eh? Wut's the big idea? Who are thee, anyway, eh? Who?

BILL: B-Bill —

HAMBULL: Eh? Who? Wut caper art up to i' my shed, eh?

BILL: Manager sent me.

HAMBULL: Eh? Wut art slummockin' round my bench for?

BILL: I told you. Charlie Burgess, t'manager sent me. He sent me to you for you to find a woman for me, to learn me weavin' afore I can go an' work as an' apprentice in t'mechanic's shop.

HAMBULL: Wut the hell does Chey Burgess think he's on? (*Pause*) Anyway, tha means 'teach'. Learning is wut tha does thyself, if tha has sense enough. Right (*shouts*) Hetty! Hetty!

    Signals for her to come to him — large wave of arm and a downward point to his feet. HETTY *enters.*

HAMBULL (*to* BILL): I'm putting thee wi' Hetty Dale here, see tha does wut she tells thee — or else tha'll have me to contend with.

HAMBULL *moves away.* HETTY *smiles at* BILL
who smiles back. Suddenly HAMBULL *returns.*

HAMBULL (*close to* BILL): How old are you?
BILL: Fourteen and a bit.
HAMBULL: Thy first job?
BILL: Aye.
HAMBULL (*gripping his arm*): Me an' thee, lad, we'll be
the only two men in the entire shed. A shedful of
women, see. (*Taps* BILL*'s shoulder with spanner.*) I'm
t'gaffer here, an' let me give thee a tip — no wenching!
I won't stand for it.

Pause. BILL *swallows,* HAMBULL *quickly releases
him and disappears.*

HETTY: Eh up, luv. (BILL *starts — he has been staring
after* HAMBULL) Ee, you look a bit sick you do. Here,
have a sup of water. (*She goes to mug and jug; pours.*)
If you don't mind drinking out of my mug.

*He takes the mug from her and is obviously shaking
as he drinks.*

HETTY (*smiling*): Here, let me help you with your jacket.
(*She takes his jacket off.*) That's a new shirt that, isn't it?
BILL: Yes.
HETTY (*unbuttoning his sleeves and rolling them up*): I
bet your mam bought that for you, didn't she? Your
first working shirt.
BILL (*relaxing a bit*): Yes.
HETTY: Come on then. You to go on t'looms next to
mine. (*She goes*)
BILL (*to audience*): It seemed to me that Hetty moved
like — a sprite. She darted about the alleyway from one
loom to another — and I followed — slowfooted. Often
I'd lose sight of her, when suddenly from between the
reeds the two green eyes, laughing and bright, would

startle me. Of an afternoon, especially Friday, she'd start singing. Her voice fascinated me, for she could pitch it so that it rose with a tormenting sweetness above the din of the machinery. After her wash before going home she looked very pretty, with her smooth hair gleaming, and delicate skin. And sometimes she changed her blouse and came to work in her best coat, and then I could hardly keep my eyes off her.

Enter HETTY *with coat on ready for home.*

BILL: Going to meet your boy?

HETTY: Pooh — if you haven't got a boy by my age, you never will have.

BILL: You're not that old!

HETTY: I am, luv, an' never been kicked, kissed or run over.

BILL: Eee I wouldn't ha' thought it. I mean — that you were — old.

HETTY *laughs and goes.*

BILL: It was Hetty made the job bearable for me — all day long in the same narrow alley, two feet wide and ten feet long; our heads bent together over the same cloth, our bodies brushing by each other every minute or two, our hands touching — and when I felt her soft hand against mine it seemed the sight slipped from my eyes and I couldn't see what the cotton was doing. Sometimes we would kiss the same shuttle. I'd have to press my mouth to the tiny hole in the shuttle and suck and suck without the cotton coming through, then Hetty would just touch it with her lips and the thread would spring out.

Noise increases, lights fade.

Scene Thirteen

Beneath a street lamp. BILL *strolls on, hands in pockets,*
   ELLA *follows behind.*

ELLA: How's work? Do you like it?

BILL: Champion.

ELLA: I could tell. (*Pause*) Which way are we going?

BILL: I don't know. I might have to go in, in a bit.

ELLA (*pause*): I wish you'd spit it out.

BILL: What?

ELLA: Whatever's on your mind. You've done nowt but
   moan tonight.

BILL: I don't know Ella — I'm just wondering what's
   going to happen.

ELLA: When?

BILL: When you start work.

ELLA: Th' whole place'll probably come out on strike in
   protest.

BILL: No, with you and me I mean.

ELLA: We can go out a bit can't we? My mam's said I can
   have a penny in the shilling, so we can go to the pictures
   or somewhere. Instead of hiding up back entries . . .

BILL: Ah, will you want to though?

ELLA: What? Carry on hiding up entries?

BILL: No! Still want to see me?

ELLA: Why shouldn't I?

BILL: Work changes folk, you know.

ELLA: Tell you what. You're on six to two shift, I'm on
   eight till six. Why don't you wait for me? You know the
   cemetry gate just opposite th' Wild Goose Mill? Wait
   there. Just after six.

BILL: If you like.

ELLA: You'll see, I'll be just the same when I come out
   as when I went in.

   He goes, she follows.

Scene Fourteen

The weaving shed. The lights change and the noise resumes to indicate that we are back in the weaving shed. BILL *takes off his coat and rolls up his sleeves as he talks.*

BILL: One thing that eluded me was the 'weaver's knot'. This was a knot tied in a special way, to repair a broken end in the warp, and me, with my thick fingers, I couldn't master it. The times I wished I had the quickness of Spadger — he could do anything with his hands — or his feet. Touching the warp was like I had thick bandages on all me fingers.

Enter HETTY.

HETTY: Gone again?
BILL: Yes.
HETTY: Here.

He kneels, she brings one arm over each of his shoulders and takes his hands. Her cheek touches his — he is totally flummoxed by this.

HETTY: You'll never make a weaver till you can tie the weaver's knot. Let your fingers go loose — go on. That's it. Now — look — are you looking? (*He nods*) That end over there, then round — through — under and — got it —
BILL: It's too fiddly. I can't hold the ends.
HETTY: Look — try it — I'll just watch.

She leans her hands on his shoulders and watches as he attempts to tie the knot. Round, through, under, and . . .

HETTY (*laughing*): Ee, luv, you've done it — you've tied your first weaver's knot. (*She kneels beside him.*) Here — you deserve a reward. (*She takes his face in both her hands and kisses him on the mouth.* BILL *stares — she holds his face and smiles — then —*) Oh Hetty — you didn't ought to have done it . . .

She stands — straightens herself — BILL *watches her.*
Enter HAMBULL.

HAMBULL (*watches for a moment*): How's the young
   'un, Hetty. Weaned him yet, have you?
HETTY: Eh?
HAMBULL: I'd o' thought he'd be ont' looms of his own
   by this.
BILL: I could an' all, given half the chance.
HAMBULL: Oh, you could, could you? What d'you think
   Hetty?
HETTY: Suit yourself.
HAMBULL: All right me young 'master'. Take them two
   looms at th' end next to Hetty's. (*He goes*)
BILL: What've I done?
HETTY: Go on, you'll be all right. I'll still be able to give
   you a lift. (*She goes*)

   BILL *watches after her, wipes his hands with a cloth.*
   Fade noise of looms; change lights.

Scene Fifteen

In front of the gable end. BILL *remains in position. Enter*
   SPADGER.

SPADGER: Did you hear about that chap in the paper
   who poisoned his wife with a razor?
BILL: Aye, he gave her arsenic.
SPADGER: Good eh? Arse a nick.
BILL: How's the snuffy?
SPADGER: Haven't you heard?
BILL: What?
SPADGER: They've had to let me go.
BILL: Laid off?
SPADGER: In a manner of speaking. You know I was
   telling you about my feet the other day — you know,
   how they wouldn't take me into the yard?

BILL: Aye.

SPADGER: Well I went to work next day and Albert Wimpole, you know, the minder in my shed —

BILL: You never told him?!

SPADGER: I'm not the one to keep worritin about what lies to tell — you know that Bill. Just refer back to the truth, that's my motto. So I told him — I didn't come to work because me feet wouldn't let me.

BILL: And what did he say?

SPADGER: 'My feet', he said, 'have not wanted to enter the mill yard for the past forty years, but I've had to make them. I'm sorry, Spadger,' he said, 'but I'll hatta sack you. I mean just think if the word got round — there wouldn't be a soul in this damn place tomorrow. Temperature at ninety, humidity damn near a hundred — who'd work in a place like this in his right senses?'

BILL: He's got a point.

SPADGER: Oh, I don't blame him. Folk in authority've got to keep up appearances.

BILL: S'ppose they have.

SPADGER: Done me a favour really. I got a job in the pit.

BILL: You haven't?

SPADGER: Aye. Pony lad.

BILL: I didn't think you'd be workin' in an office.

SPADGER: Give over! This is a real job. I'm not coddin' Bill, but I love it.

BILL: And your dad's letting you?

SPADGER: Fait accompli, mate. It's a grand job when you get used to it. What you call a man's job.

BILL: You've got a bit to go yet, Spadger.

SPADGER: Don't be clever; it doesn't suit you.

BILL: Sorry, Spadger.

SPADGER: Here, but I'm not kiddin' — the chaps you work with are right toffs. You'd never get me working on top again. I'm going to be a coalminer to my dyin' day.

BILL: I thought you were going to be a footballer.

Lights fade.

Scene Sixteen

The weaving shed. BILL *takes two mugs from workbench.*
Enter HETTY.

BILL: Cocoa's here, Hetty.
HETTY: Thanks, love.

Pause, they drink.

BILL (*reaching in pocket*): I brought you some chocolate.
Fruit and nut.
HETTY: Again?
BILL (*laughs*): Yes.
HETTY: Not this morning, love, I don' feel like eating
anything.
BILL: Are you all right? You haven't looked yourself
lately, Hetty. An' I never hear you singing now. Have
you just come over funny?
HETTY (*smiles*): Come here. (BILL *goes to her*) Closer.
(*he does so*) I'm going to have a baby.

BILL *stares at her, speechless.*

HETTY: Know who's the father?

BILL *shakes his head.*

HETTY (*pointing at him*): You!
BILL: Me!
HETTY: Yes — you. It must have been that day you kissed
me behind the looms. I've never felt the same since.

BILL *tries to find something to say.*

HETTY: Cross my heart, Bill, I won't tell a soul. But let it
be a lesson to you.

She laughs and goes. BILL *is left amazed.*

66

BILL (*to audience*): Those last months Hetty had spent more time with me than with anybody and she'd never been out of my thoughts, and I'd kissed her — or she'd kissed me — and all that couldn't mean nothing!

Enter HETTY *hurriedly.*

HETTY (*whisper*): Eh, Eddie Hambull!
BILL: Eh?

Enter HAMBULL.

HAMBULL: How long does it take thee to drink a simple cup of cocoa? I've had to shut your loom down — two flamin' shuttles stuck in, bladderhead! D'you think I've no more to do than wet-nurse thee? Sort it out will you, 'fore I lose my temper. (*He goes.*)
HETTY (*seeing* BILL'*s anger*): Leave him. I'll help you sort it out.
BILL: Why does he hate me?
HETTY: It's just his way. Come on. Give us a lift with these weights, an' I'll keep an eye out for him.

They go and lift weights from beneath work bench. BILL *lifts and goes to leave with weights.* HETTY *groans behind him and sinks to one knee.*

BILL (*turning*): What's up, Hetty?
HETTY: I've hurt me, love. Help me round to my box.

BILL *supports* HETTY *to sit on box next to bench. She is doubled up.*

BILL: Shall I fetch woman from t'welfare room?
HETTY: No — go an' tell Eddie.
BILL: Who — Hambull?
HETTY: Yes. He's gaffer.

BILL *stands up — hesitates. Enter* DELIA.

HETTY: Bill! Will you do as you're told?!

BILL *goes.*

DELIA: Eee, Hetty, what's up? (HETTY *cries out*) Are you hurt? What Hetty? (*Goes to her*)

Enter HAMBULL *and* BILL.

HAMBULL: Wut's up? Wut have you done? Liftin' flamin' weights — have you no more sense? (*to* BILL) Hy thee — dash off to Joe Key an' tell him to have the firm's car ready. Say one of my weavers has been taken bad.

BILL *goes.* HAMBULL *lifts* HETTY *and with his arm round her hurries off.*

HAMBULL: Hold on, love, hold on. We'll have you in t'infirmary in no time. (*They go.* DELIA *hurries after.*)

Enter BILL.

BILL: The only reason I went to work the next day was that I was drawn to the job and the alley between the looms. My eyes kept getting drawn to her four looms, standing in strange idleness, and I kept thinking I saw her there.

Burst of loom noise. Enter DELIA *and another girl. They carry mugs of cocoa — one each and one for* BILL.

DELIA (*to* BILL): Cocoa love.

BILL *takes his cocoa and moves to one side. The girls talk.*

GIRL (*pause*): Last night at ten o'clock in the infirmary.
DELIA: So I heard. Stillborn.
GIRL: But she's all right.

BILL *looks towards them.*

DELIA: That Hambull!
GIRL: It were a lucky let-off for him!

DELIA: Fancy! And it would have been his first.
GIRL: At his age?
DELIA: Wife's an invalid.
GIRL: Men always come off best.
DELIA: Women has to pay.

Enter HAMBULL. *The women see him, put down their drinks and hurry off.* BILL *stares at him for a moment and moves as if to speak to* HAMBULL. *Changes his mind then moves to leave.*

HAMBULL: Where are you off to?
BILL: I'm leaving.
HAMBULL: Wut?
BILL: I'm chucking it. I've had enough.

Pause. HAMBULL *takes* BILL's *arm. Leads him downstage and speaks quietly to him, for the first time.*

HAMBULL: I suppose it's over my shouting at thee yesterday. Lad, thy'll punish thyself all through life.
BILL: How come?
HAMBULL: Tha takes things to heart. I'm same myself. (*Pause*) I've just had a thing happen to me that I can't tell thee or nob'dy else about, but I will say this — I've suffered the loss of a life's hope. I were young yesterday — now I'm an old man.

Pause: they look at each other. HAMBULL *breaks the mood suddenly.*

HAMBULL: And where art going, lad?
BILL: Navy. I'm turned fifteen nearly.
HAMBULL: Then tha'll be going to sea.
BILL: Aye, to sea.

Pause.

HAMBULL: There's nowt here for me. I wish — I wish I were coming wi' thee.

BILL: Aye — (HAMBULL *holds out his hand — they shake hands*) I wish you were, Eddie.

BILL *goes.* HAMBULL *stands alone. Slow blackout.*

Scene Seventeen

A navy recruiting station. BILL *stands centre stage taking his shirt off. A woman* DOCTOR *in a white coat waits until his shirt is off, then listens to his chest.*

DOCTOR: Don't be nervous, there's nothing to worry about. You've passed the interview. The medical's only a formality.

BILL *nods.*

DOCTOR (*listens*): Have you been running?

BILL *shakes his head.*

DOCTOR: Are you breathing?

BILL *shakes his head.*

DOCTOR: You die if you don't breathe, you know. Trying to give it up, are we?

BILL *manages a faint smile.*

DOCTOR: Ummm. (DOCTOR *stands back and scratches her head.*) That heart of yours is beating like a tom-tom drum. I think you'd better come back in a year's time — when you've calmed down a bit.

BILL: Pardon?

DOCTOR: Next!

BILL: But I've told everybody I'm joining the navy!

DOCTOR: We'll see you this time next year. Thank you — you can dress outside.

DOCTOR *writes,* BILL *leaves dumbfounded. Blackout.*

Scene Eighteen

A street corner. Enter FELIX, ERNIE *and* PONGO.

FELIX: Blasted string on my apron broke and yard bobby spotted my bulging pockets!

PONGO: Crikey!

ERNIE: Oranges again were it, Felix?

FELIX: Aye, seventeen of the flamers. 'An example has to be made', he said, 'of somebody or other. There's too much thieving going on in this yard.'

ERNIE: It aren't thieving. It's perks.

FELIX: He made me lay every blessed one of 'em out on table.

PONGO: What did you say to him?

FELIX: Nothing. I didn't say nothing. I were too frightened.

ERNIE: 'Anything you say may be used in evidence against you.'

FELIX: Right. So off he went to get his mate as a witness, — and locked me in just to make sure — with th' evidence.

PONGO: Ooh, my dad'd kill me!

FELIX: No escape. There I was locked in with the evidence there before me on the table.

ERNIE: Ruined for life.

FELIX: At least. Anyway — suddenly, up pipes this little voice inside my head.

ERNIE: Voice?

FELIX: Clear as a bell. 'Eat 'em,' it said.

PONGO: Eat 'em?

FELIX: Aye — eat 'em. 'And then the evidence will be gone,' it said. 'But be quick about it.' I thought for a second, snatched an orange, peeled it in a jiff and squashed it into my mouth.

PONGO: Think of that juice!

FELIX: I was just about to squirt out the pips when up pipes this voice again. 'No!' it thundered. 'Eh?' I said. 'You have to swallow them too!' 'The pips?' I said. 'Aye, peel an' all.'

71

PONGO: No.

FELIX: 'Don't bother to chew,' said the voice. 'It's a race against time!' I took out my penknife, slashed the oranges into chunks and gulped them down, hand over fist you might say. By the time the yard bobby was turning the key in the lock I was consuming the final piece of the seventeen oranges.

ERNIE: I'd have bust!

FELIX: 'This is him,' says the bobby to his mate, 'I caught him with his pockets ramjam full of oranges.' He looked at the table. 'Hi, where are they?' he cried. 'Whew,' sniffed his mate, 'I can smell 'em.'

PONGO: I bet he could.

FELIX: Still, I kept my mouth shut. He looked high and low but he found no trace of an orange. Finally he figured out what must have happened. 'Seventeen!!' he kept murmuring, 'Big 'uns at that — how has he managed it?' I just looked at him — lips sealed. So he had to let me go — no evidence to keep me in charge you see.

ERNIE: Eh — you should have sued him for wrongful detention.

FELIX: Give over — anyway, it was days and days before I could really stand still and think things out, because those seventeen oranges — peel, pips and all — kept working away in my inside something shocking.

ERNIE: I would have sued him for thousands.

PONGO: I love an orange I do.

FELIX: Thought of 'em makes me head for nearest privy.

PONGO: You've made me hungry now. What say we go down to Ditchfield's for an hot pie?

ERNIE: Fair enough.

FELIX: Did I ever tell you about Dickie Flitt and the hot pie?

PONGO: Are we going?

FELIX: All right. Living two doors from me when I was a lad was a lad called Dickie Flitt.

ERNIE: I remember.

FELIX: He was my closest pal at the time . . . (*They are gone*)

    Enter BILL *and* SPADGER.

BILL: It's all right for you. How can I face the world wi' them all knowing how the Navy chucked me out?

SPADGER: You'll rot stuck away in your house.

BILL: What's the alternative?

SPADGER: Come down pit an' work wi' me. Eh, wut about that for a good idea? Who wants to work int' rotten Navy anyroad?

BILL: No use, Spadge, my mam and dad wouldn't let me on account of my dad working down pit as well.

SPADGER: They all say that, yet they all keep working down pit themselves. But I'll tell you something, you've got better mates working down pit than anywhere else I know. Far better than those who work on top. There's danger see, an' where there's danger men allus pull together. Why, I wouldn't even swop my pit pony for some of the folks I've worked with. I give him a nice bit of currant cake every shift — he loves it. So listen — say I get you a start —

BILL: But my dad says —

SPADGER: Never mind your dad — for the moment. Your mam is the one that matters. Dads are nothing. You know that. I know she'll give way to you — she always does in the long run. If you keep at her. So if I get you a start along side me wi' the pit ponies — you've only got to go home once all black from the coal dirt and then it's what they call —

BILL: Fait accompli —

SPADGER: That's it. It'll be over an' done with an' no use arguing.

BILL: Will you just let me sleep on it for a few days, Spadge —

Enter MICHAEL. *He carries a suitcase.*

SPADGER: Hey — your Michael!

BILL *turns and looks.* MICHAEL *stops.*

SPADGER: Howgo Mike? We're right fain to see you,
  aren't we Bill?
MICHAEL: Is me mam in?
BILL: She's never out is she?
MICHAEL: I think you've grown, Bill. Been using my
  weights?
BILL (*smiles*): Haven't damaged 'um.
MICHAEL: What about my bike?
BILL: In the shed. Daren't take it out in case our mam
  got to thinking about — where've you been?
MICHAEL: Liverpool.
SPADGER: What's it like?
MICHAEL: All right.
BILL: Have you brought Nan back with you?
MICHAEL: Nan's left me. Took the baby. (*Pause*) Can't
  blame her. No work — an' me. She hasn't come to her
  mother's has she?
BILL: Haven't seen her.

  Pause.

SPADGER: I'll take your case. You run ahead and
  warn your mother, Bill. (SPADGER *takes case,* BILL
  pauses for a second then goes.) How did you get here,
  Mike?
MICHAEL: Cadged a lift on a lorry.
SPADGER: Did you?

  They go.

74

Scene Nineteen

Spadger's Mother's parlour. Centre stage, SPADGER *is curled up asleep on a rug. Enter his* MOTHER, *followed by* BILL.

MOTHER: He's in here, love. Sshh!

> *They tiptoe over to where* SPADGER *sleeps and stand either side of him.*

BILL: Is he all right?

MOTHER: He was that weary when he got home today — he couldn't eat his dinner.

BILL (*slight laugh*): I've never seen him so still.

MOTHER: He's in another world, love. 'Can I have five minutes in front of fire?' he says to me, and the next thing he was right out.

BILL: Dreaming o' pit ponies and tubs o' coal.

MOTHER: Poor lad, he's dead beat.

SPADGER (*opening his eyes*): Who's dead beat?

MOTHER: Bill's here to call for you, love.

SPADGER (*rising with a groan*): Howgo, Bill?

BILL: All right, Spadge.

SPADGER: I'm getting old. I think I'll wash me.

MOTHER: Have your dinner first, love. I've kept it warm for you in th' oven.

SPADGER: All right, mam.

MOTHER (*going*): It's potato pie. Might be a bit dry by this.

SPADGER: Where you off?

BILL: Nowhere.

SPADGER: Anybody out?

BILL: Few o' the lads. We could have a game o' knock-up wi' them.

SPADGER: Have you no finer feelings? Look at me!

BILL: Or we could just go scrounging round, see what we can see.

75

Enter MOTHER *with pie dish and two pint pots of tea.*

MOTHER: I've made you a nice mug of tea to go with it, and Billy can have a drink with you.

SPADGER: Can I eat it in front of fire, mam?

MOTHER: Long as you don't mention it to your dad. You know what he's like.

SPADGER (*eating*): It's very tasty, mam.

MOTHER: I'm slipping down to Mrs. Doughty's before your dad gets in. Will you be all right?

SPADGER: Don't you worry, mam.

MOTHER: See he eats it all, Billy, will you? Tara.

BILL: Tara, Mrs. Chadwick.

She goes. Pause.

BILL: Looks more than a bit dry to me, Spadge.

SPADGE: Say nought about it. It's very easy to hurt her feelings.

He continues to eat. BILL *drinks tea. Pause.*

BILL: You know when I was working in t'weaving shed?

SPADGER: Mmm.

BILL: This woman I was working with —

SPADGER: Hetty Dale.

BILL: How did you know her name?

SPADGER: You told me.

BILL: I don't remember telling you. (*Pause.* SPADGER *shrugs*) Anyway — this one morning she sent to t'mechanic's shop for some grease. On my way I spotted this iron ladder. It went up water tower. Something came over me and I had to climb it. Two minutes and I was right up in the air. The breeze went right into my throat. I was — you know escaped from the sweat and the din and the —

SPADGER: The orders of work.

BILL: Right. But then — I held back. I looked at my two feet on the ladder. It was like one foot was climbing up

76

and th' other was hanging back ready to climb down. One foot up — one foot down (*Pause*) I just — keep remembering it. (*Pause*) I've made up my mind — I'd like to come down pit wi' you.

SPADGER: Good lad you! I'll have a word with the under-manager — see if you can start Monday morning. I'll ask him to put you on the day shift alongside me.

BILL: Oh, luv'ly, Spadge.

SPADGER: Now register this — I'll give you a whistle outside your front door at five minutes past five. Get your mum to give you a call at half-past four. We catch the quarter past five tram outside the tripe shop and we get off at Four Lane Ends. Oh ah, whatever tha does, bring a piece of cake for the pony — he must have his taste o' cake — currant cake preferred. He's very fussy.

BILL: Leave it to me. I'll bring him a big piece. My mum always bakes on a Sunday.

Pause. SPADGER *drinks his tea.*

BILL: Not like you to be tired Spadger.

SPADGER: Never mind me; will you remember what to do on Monday?

BILL: Course.

SPADGER: That's what I wanted to hear, me old son. Here, tha can put this dish into soak an' I'll get me wash.

They rise and leave.

Scene Twenty

A street corner. JIMMY, ERNIE, BASHER, *and* PONGO.

JIMMY (*to* PONGO): Come on, roll thy trouser leg up!

PONGO: No!

ERNIE: Do it, will you?

PONGO: No.

JIMMY: It won't hurt.

ERNIE: An' it's got to be done.

JIMMY: We all do it, Pongo.

PONGO: Aye, an' scream your heads off in t'process.

ERNIE: No we don't.

JIMMY: That's just cod.

ERNIE: It only hurts when a novice has a go. We're experts, aren't we lads?

Agreement 'Course we are'; 'Yes'.

PONGO: But I haven't got any.

ERNIE: When did you last look?

JIMMY: Bet you haven't had those keks off since we went swimming at school.

PONGO: Course I have.

ERNIE: When?

PONGO: In t'privy.

JIMMY: Not right off — only round your knees.

PONGO: Same thing.

JIMMY: Look, Pongo. Do you, or don't you, wipe under your machine?

PONGO: Course.

JIMMY: And is the floor oily, or is it not?

PONGO: Yes.

JIMMY: You've got them then. Hold him Ernie.

JIMMY *and* ERNIE *grab* PONGO's *arms.*

PONGO: You're hurting me.

JIMMY: I haven't started yet!

PONGO: All right, all right. Let me go then.

They release him; he tries to run but they grab him.

JIMMY: Tell you what, tell you what. Pongo — you can do mine.

PONGO: Eh?

JIMMY (*rolling up trouser leg*): Come on, I'll be guinea pig.

PONGO: I don't like.

JIMMY: I aren't going to drop stone stiff dead!

PONGO: All right. What do I do?

JIMMY: Come over here for a start. (PONGO *approaches*) Now look at my leg. What can you see?

PONGO: Hairs.

JIMMY: Between th' hairs.

PONGO: Oh yeah!!

JIMMY: Grubs they are, Pongo.

PONGO: Alive!?

JIMMY: Not real grubs y'pillock! Blackhead grubs. Now you take your finger and thumb. Not ont' same hand — finger off one hand, thumb off th'other — place either side and squeeze. Go on, go on — (*grits teeth in pain*)

PONGO (*delighted*): Oh yeah — it's coming out.

JIMMY (*relaxing*): See, it didn't hurt.

Enter FELIX *eating a butty.*

PONGO: Can I do another?

JIMMY: Be my guest. Then I'll do you.

FELIX: Howgo lads?

ERNIE: What you got, Felix?

FELIX (*swaggering*): Pork stuffing butty.

ERNIE: Pay day at your house?

FELIX: We allus have a quarter of pork on a Friday.

ERNIE: Show off — you're nothing else.

JIMMY: Reckon Wanderers'll be at Wembley again this year, Felix?

FELIX: Eh? Wut Jimmy? I was just showing Ernie this pork stuffing butty. Beats a sauce butty any time.

JIMMY: I'd eat it quick if I were you — 'fore you get it grappled from you be an hoard o' starving lads. You can watch Pongo working on my leg whilst you dine.

FELIX: Good idea, Jimmy. (*He goes and watches*)

JIMMY: What's your opinion about Wanderers then?

ERNIE: They've sold David Jack to Arsenal now, haven't they? What's left wi'out David Jack?

Enter SPADGER *and* BILL.

FELIX: Ah but you don't make a team out o' one man!

JIMMY: What's your opinion, Spadge? About Wanderers' chances for Wembley?

SPADGER: Kick an' rush merchants!

FELIX: Eh?

SPADGER: They're playing football as though the ball was their deadly enemy — you can see it in their faces — they belt it as hard as they can. Look at Bob Thropper — he don't kick it — he attempts premeditated murder! Now David Jack — he played football as though that ball were his best friend.

BILL: Like you do, Spadge.

SPADGER: As though he loved it.

JIMMY: You've got a point, Spadge.

Lads deep in thought. Pause. Enter SIM DALT.

ERNIE: Hey — Sim Dalt!!

PONGO: 'Lo Mr. Dalt.

SIM: Hello lad.

PONGO: Thought you'd left Bolton.

SIM: No.

PONGO: Only — when th' amusement arcade closed, I heard you'd left.

SIM: Miss me, do you?

PONGO: I were there that night you stopped three shots from Bob Thropper.

ERNIE: And I was, Mr. Dalt. Everybody heard about it.

JIMMY: Why did you shut up shop then?

PONGO: Don't be so forward, Jimmy.

SIM: I'm looking for a lad called Chadwick.

PONGO: Spadger!

SIM: That's the one.

ERNIE: This is Spadger, Mr. Dalt. Here, Spadge, this is Mr. Dalt.

SPADGER: How do, Mr. Dalt?

SIM: Was that you playing for Witton Street Sunday School team a week last Tuesday?

SPADGER: I had a game for them, yes.

BILL: You didn't tell me.

SPADGER: I was just helping them out. They were a man down.

SIM: One o' my scouts speaks very high of you, young man.

JIMMY: From th' amusement arcade?

SIM: From Bolton Wanderers, laddie. When you buy enough shares they make you a director.

ERNIE: Flappin' Nora!! I wondered where you'd gone.

BILL: And you want Spadge?

PONGO: Bolton Wanderers, Spadge! First Division!

SIM: Wondered if you'd fancy a trial. For the nursery team. If you get in we give you a go in the A team, then, if you're any good, reserves: then maybe first team.

ERNIE: Flappin' Nora!!

SIM: We're looking for a centre forward.

JIMMY: Bob Thropper's centre forward.

SIM: Not any more he's not. He's looking for a quiet little pub somewhere. Like I said to him, 'Centre forwards, I can buy 'em and sell 'em. Least I can sell 'em.' Wut say, lad, will you give it a go?

SPADGER: I'll hatta borrow a pair of boots off somebody. Sole's come off mine.

BILL: I think I've got a pair not too bad.

SPADGER: Have you?

BILL: You can have 'em.

SPADGER: Just the job. I might have to put an extra pair of socks in 'em, but no more.

SIM: Week Sat'dy morning at the ground. Ten o'clock. I'll have the papers ready for you to sign — if you shape up that is. Tara lads.

LADS: Tara Mr. Dalt.

SIM DALT *goes.*

JIMMY: Wait till I tell me dad.

ERNIE: He's got you lined up for a replacement, Spadge.

PONGO: I knew this'd happen.

ERNIE: Spadger Chadwick, the new David Jack.

JIMMY: And to think — he'll get his start in your boots, Bill.

ERNIE: Flappin' Nora!!

SPADGER: It's only a trial.

JIMMY: Only!!

SPADGER: Hold on, lads. I like working down pit. I'm not so sure I'd go daft about playing football for a living, as much as I like the game.

JIMMY: Wut? Art having a brain seize-up me old son? Bugger pit!

SPADGER: And look what he said about poor old Thropper — bought and sold.

JIMMY: Ah, but that goes back to when they were kids — it were a personal point.

BILL: The goalkeeper's revenge.

JIMMY: Right! Nowt to do wi' you, Spadge.

SPADGER: Still, I don't know.

ERNIE: Hey! You could slip us free tickets for Wembley. Think of it!

JIMMY: I could tell me grandchildren how I once played footer with the legendary Spadger Chadwick. Down our alley wi' a pig's bladder.

ERNIE: Wut say we go and spread the news?

SPADGER: Hold on —

JIMMY: Right. (*going*) Bags I have first go.

ERNIE: Second.

They leave noisily.

SPADGER: Hold on. (*Pause, he looks at* BILL) Ta for the loan of the boots, Bill.

BILL: I'm right pleased, Spadge.

SPADGER: Are you?

BILL: Wish I were coming with you, that's all.

SPADGER: I'm not going anywhere.

BILL: Different world though i'nt it?

SPADGER: No, you don't get me. I'll go for the trial —
but — play football for a living? I don't want to, Bill.

BILL: Chuck up the chance? You could — I don't know —
all the things you could see.

SPADGER: What for? I like it here. (*pause*) Fancy a game
of pontoon in our back parlour?

BILL: What about the lads?

SPADGER: Let 'um have their fun. They'll find out the
rest in good time.

SPADGER *goes.* BILL *follows on gloomily.*

Scene Twenty-One

A patch of waste ground. SAMMY *alone, holding a taut
kite string and looking away into the distance. Enter*
BILL.

BILL (*joining* SAMMY *and looking along the string*):
Good lad, Sammy.

SAM: Her's pulling a bit to the left.

BILL: She can take it.

SAM: Can tha' see her?

BILL: Aye, but only just. Still winding out, Sammy?

SAM: I want her out of sight.

Pause.

BILL: I've lost her, I think she's gone. Can't see a speck
of her, Sammy.

SAM: We'll just give her an extra yard. Got the time, Bill?

BILL: All but seven.

SAM: Flappin' Nora. I've got to go to the outdoor licence
for my dad's allowance. Would tha' hold on till I come
back?

BILL: Hold the kite, Sam?

SAM: Aye, she'll be all right. Steady as an eagle but pullin'. Just hold on an' I'll be back in five minutes.

BILL takes the string and SAM rushes off. Pause as BILL holds on. Enter ELLA.

BILL (*seeing her*): I'm just holding Sammy's kite for him till he comes back. He's gone to the off-licence for his dad's allowance. He asked me to hold it.

Pause.

ELLA: Is it pullin' hard?

BILL: Yes, tidy hard. Would — d'you want to feel at how it's pullin'?

ELLA: If you'll hold it wi' me.

BILL: All right. (*He holds out the kite stick*) Come on, get hold.

ELLA: I'm frightened of it. It might get away.

BILL: I'll hold with you.

She joins him and they hold on together. Pause.

BILL: Why did you never meet me that time?

ELLA: I tried to tell you the other day.

BILL: I stood there and you just went by with the girls laughing.

ELLA: I came back an' you weren't there. I had to walk with them so they wouldn't know. I thought you wouldn't want them to know. I turned round at Enty's shop and came back. I waited till twenty-five past eight.

BILL: But Ella — you went by —

ELLA: I looked for you every night after work.

BILL: How did I know that?

ELLA: You could easily have seen me if you'd looked. I don't even know where you work now.

BILL: Why didn't you tell me the other day?

ELLA: What? While you were with Spadger?

BILL: No —

ELLA: No, I'm a mucky doffer, aren't I? A dirty card-room girl!

BILL: Ella!

ELLA: You wouldn't want a smelly doffer.

BILL: Ella don't. Sam's coming.

ELLA: I can see, an' I don't bloody well care — I'm sick of trying to work out what it is you want me to do — (*She goes*)

BILL (*quietly*): Oh, Ella —

    Enter SAMMY.

SAMMY: How's she been pullin' Bill?

BILL (*handing over string*): Strong. Her's been pulling strong. Can tha' feel them flecks o' rain, Sammy?

SAMMY: Aye, I thought I did feel a drop then.

BILL: Tha'd better pull in then, eh?

SAMMY: I don't like having a kite up, wi'out going bare stick.

BILL: You're not letting off more, Sammy?

SAMMY: Aye! It's half-hearted else. You just watch her take it. (*unwinds*) Only a few more yards, bare stick, then wind in.

BILL: That's enough, Sammy. (*Suddenly the string flies off and away*) The string — grab it!

    They rush hopelessly — perhaps falling over.

BILL: No use, Sam — it'll be falling now — miles away — like a great broken bird.

SAMMY: The last I'll ever see of her, Bill.

BILL: Ee, I'm sorry, Sammy.

SAMMY: I'll never understand how that string weren't tied on to the winding-on stick. I've never known it. It's the first thing I do — tie it on. I must have forgot. (*He picks up the stick.*) Here Bill, that's a good winding-on stick. Thee have it. (*Pause*) Go on.

BILL: Ta, Sammy.

SAMMY (*pauses looking up*): I wonder where she fell?

BILL: Oh, o'er Pennine Chain, Sammy. Aye, I'll bet, and beyond.

SAMMY: Her pulled a bit to the left, but I wouldn't have altered her. (*Pause*) Oh, Bill —

BILL: Aye?

SAMMY: Say naught about it.

BILL: Not a word, if you don't want me to.

SAMMY: Ta.

SAMMY *goes,* BILL *watches him go. Lights fade.*

Scene Twenty-Two

In front of Bill's house. Enter LAD *with book. Pause. Enter* BILL.

LAD: Er — (*Holds out book*)

BILL: What would I want with this?

LAD: You collect books, don't you?

BILL: You make 'em sound like cigarette cards.

LAD: You know what I mean.

BILL (*reads*): *The Little Red Hen.* I'm a bit past that.

LAD: They got some of the pictures in colour.

BILL: It's words I go in for in general. Anyroad, says here it were a prize for you.

LAD: Poem Learning Competition. 'The North Wind Doth Blow'.

BILL: Very good.

LAD: Off by heart.

BILL: I shouldn't give it away if I were you.

Enter ERNIE *and* SAMMY.

LAD: What's this about you getting a start at pit?

BILL: Yes, Monday morning, with Spadger.

LAD: Wish I could go.

BILL: You're too little yet.

LAD: You have to be little if you're a miner. You want to watch you don't bang your head.

BILL: Don't you be cheeky.

LAD: Or get gassed. (*Runs off*)

   BILL *laughs and watches him go.*

ERNIE: Hast tha' not heard then?

BILL: Heard what?

ERNIE: Bout old Spadger?

BILL: What?

ERNIE: He's getten hurt. Trapped between tubs o' coal or summat.

SAMMY: Some o' the chaps fetched him home couple of hours since.

ERNIE: Will you be going in d'you think, Bill?

BILL: What?

ERNIE: The undertaker's been and gone. (*Pause*) Sammy doesn't want to.

BILL: Spadger!

SAMMY: I'd — I'd sooner remember him as he was.

ERNIE: His mother will be expecting you though. She might be hurt if you didn't go in.

   Pause.

ERNIE: I just saw his dad go in with some jugs of beer. Most of street's in there. Sammy's mum's looking after the young 'uns.

BILL: The other lads in?

ERNIE: Yeah. I was going but — came back for Sammy. Can you talk any sense into him, Bill?

BILL: I don't know — er — you worked with him, Sam. It'll be expected.

   Pause.

SAMMY: I heard him scream Bill. Turned mi blood cold for a minute.

BILL: Were you by him?

SAMMY: Not far off. Truck severed his leg. Just like breaking a matchstick in two. I swear, he couldn't have felt anything after that. One jab.

BILL: I were all fixed to meet him on Monday morning. Five past five sharp.

SAMMY: He said. I start one week, you the next.

ERNIE: Which leg were it, Sam?

SAMMY: On his left 'un.

ERNIE: By gow! He scored many a goal wi' that leg, did Spadge.

BILL: He wasn't going to go for that trial, you know. He wasn't bothered.

ERNIE: He was. He would have got in.

BILL: Preferred pit.

ERNIE: Never!

SAMMY: They made me help bury it.

BILL: You what?

ERNIE: I've heard of that. It were always the custom, you know. If a chap loses a limb it's always got to be buried there in the yard. It wouldn't be right if the leg weren't buried there — it'd be bad luck. The older chaps wouldn't feel right.

SAMMY: You don't want to let his mother hear it.

BILL: Did they mark the spot?

SAMMY: No. Nobody'll find it now. You won't tell his mam will you, Bill? It's summat private in the pit. It's not to be talked about.

ERNIE: If I'd lost a leg, I'd want to know what they'd done with it!

BILL: He can't know. (*Pause*) Do you want to come in wi' me, Sam?

Pause.

ERNIE: It's another day tomorrow, Sammy. Have I to wait or what?

SAMMY: No hurry now is there?

ERNIE: I'm working tonight. I daren't be late for clocking on, Spadger or no Spadger.

SAMMY: Well mind you don't sup too much then.

ERNIE: I'll see you in there. (*He goes*)

BILL: Hungry Sam?

SAMMY: My mam's been busy, you know, helping Mrs. Chadwick.

BILL: Yeah, you said. I was just thinking — I spent my last penny on my new pit gear. Clogs, big tea can and snap tin. I put the currant cake in for the pony in case I forgot.

SAMMY: Will you still come?

BILL: I don't know anybody down there.

SAMMY: You know me.

BILL: With Spadger taking me — I'd not thought that there'd be other people. Never crossed my mind.

SAMMY: Don't lose heart.

BILL: Hark at you — telling me I'm losing heart when you're stuck out here on your own with everybody in Spadger's house.

SAMMY: I'm not on my own! You're here.

BILL: And all your other mates are in there.

SAMMY: Aye. In't it quiet? Forgot what this street sounded like wi'out Spadger hammering a tin cap up and down.

BILL: There'll be somebody else — some other rowdy kid — while you and me're up to our eyes in pit dirt, this street'll be taken over.

SAMMY: But we'll still come here at night won't we?

BILL: For a bit, yeah. Come on — Spadger's mum makes luv'ly great thick butties, and great mugs of steaming tea. Think of that taste. Good, eh, Sam?

SAMMY: But I won't know what to say.

BILL: Don't say anything. She'll just be glad that you're there.

SAMMY: You're supposed to say you're sorry for her trouble and — say a prayer over the coffin, aren't you?

BILL: It's nearly dark, Sammy. Be thankful for that — come on.

BILL *goes and* SAMMY.

CURTAIN